King James

King James

Believe the Hype—
The LeBron James Story

Ryan Jones

St. Martin's Press ⁂ New York

www.stmartins.com

Library of Congress Cataloging-in-Publication Data

Jones, Ryan, 1973–
   King James : believe the hype : the LeBron James story / Ryan Jones.—1st U.S. ed.
      p.   cm.
   ISBN 0-312-32229-1
   1. James, LeBron.   2. Basketball players—United States—Biography.   3. High School athletes—United States—Biography.   I. Title.

GV884.J636 2003
796.323'02—dc21
[B]

2003047234

First Edition: October 2003

10   9   8   7   6   5   4   3   2   1

Foreword

Yeah, I remember the first time I met LeBron James. I was eleven years old, and we were supposed to play against each other in a rec league game, but it got canceled. Afterward, he came up, and we introduced ourselves to each other. I didn't know him, but I respected him because he was a really good player, and he seemed cool.

But before I actually met him, I played against him in another rec league game, when I was ten. Both of our teams met in the championship game, and you could just tell right there. . . . At that age, there's always one kid on the court who's better than everyone else, and he was that kid. He was just doing things that most kids that age couldn't do. Eventually, we started playing together in AAU ball. Our program didn't have a team for younger kids, so 'Bron and Sian and me were the youngest players on the team, playing with the older kids until we got a team of our own.

As long as I've known him, 'Bron's always been good, but at first, I didn't know how good. I just knew he could be a big-time Division I player. I kind of recognized it was more than that in the summer before our freshman year. We went to the AAU nationals, and he just stepped it up. He wasn't always a great shooter, but at that tournament he was knocking down jumpers, beating guys off the dribble, everything. Some of the things he was doing . . . I watched some of those games on tape earlier this year, and he was doing things a lot of high school kids couldn't do. And he was just out of eighth grade. A lot of times, he'd even surprise you while you were on the court with him.

Now everybody knows how good he is, and with everything that's happened over the past few years, people ask me if he's changed at all. To me, he really hasn't. To the outside world, he has to be careful, but to us, he's just a really laid-back, regular person, just my friend. The one thing about him, he's humble. A lot of people seem to think LeBron is arrogant, but he's not. It's okay to be a little arrogant on the court—I think you need that—because it shows that you're confident. But off the court, he's just not like that.

He had to deal with a lot of criticism sometimes, especially last season, but he handled everything pretty well because he's a good people person, and he's not a selfish person. Whenever he had a press conference, he would always mention his teammates, and we definitely appreciated it. I think that made us closer. He also takes criticism really well, and that's part of the reason he's a good player. There were a few things people said that bothered him, but he just toughed it out. When things got down, he took it out on the court. It didn't surprise me, though, because he's a winner.

The past few years were crazy for all of us. It was a lot to deal with sometimes, but I wouldn't trade it for anything. The thing that stands out the most to me is that all of us seniors, 'Bron, Sian, Willie, Romeo, and me, we were conquerors—we got three state titles, played in four state title games, and won a national championship. I think we should all take some credit for that, because we kept each other on the right path.

I'm also proud of the things we did off the court. People don't talk about it as much, but we did a lot of charity work—we didn't just play basketball and go to school, we made a difference in our community.

Now that we've all graduated, it'll be different, but I think we'll all stay tight. I'll be a freshman at the University of Akron, right down the road from Cleveland, so I figure I'll be at a lot of Cavs games. I'm looking forward to watching 'Bron in the NBA. I know a lot of top players struggle as rookies, but I think he'll be the exception to that.

And to people who ask, Why is someone writing a book about an eighteen-year-old kid? I'd just try to explain to them that books get written all the time about people who make history—and this kid's making history every day.

—DRU JOYCE III
St. Vincent–St. Mary High School
Class of 2003

King James

Prologue

They showed the highlights that night on *SportsCenter*. It wasn't the first time the high school kid from Ohio would get his shine on ESPN, and it definitely wouldn't be the last, but this time was different. It was different because the forty-five-second segment dedicated to LeBron James ignored the best play of the night. It probably had something to do with the fact that LeBron, for once, was on the wrong end of the play.

This was a Sunday, three days before Christmas 2002, and for a passionate basketball fan, there was no better place to be than Philadelphia's legendary Palestra. An ancient gym on the campus of the University of Pennsylvania, just up the hill from downtown Philly, the Palestra owns a long, rich hoops history that was about to get a little bit richer: On this night, the best high school basketball player in America was leading his team into hostile territory. Along with their knowledge and appreciation of the game, one of the many things that make Philadelphians such great basketball fans is their loyalty—as much respect as they'll give a talented out-of-town visitor, they'll never do so at the expense of one of their own. Nor will they give up that respect easily; no matter how impressive a player's reputation, in Philly, the mantra is "show and prove."

By then, LeBron James was used to high expectations, but what made this trip unique were the atmosphere—nearly nine thousand expectant, hard-to-please fans packed standing room only into the venerable Palestra—and the competition. Slated to face LeBron and his St. Vincent–St. Mary teammates was Strawberry Mansion, a local school with its own storied tradition and led by Maureece Rice, a six-foot senior who was about to become the leading scorer in Philadelphia high school history. Simply put, the sold-out gym came in demanding a showdown between the best player in America and the most prolific scorer their city had ever produced—King James, head to head with 'Reece Rice. Only one of them would get the benefit of the doubt from that crowd, and it wouldn't be LeBron.

The crowd's loyalty was established before tip-off: Upon introductions, LeBron heard a roughly fifty-fifty mix of applause (from those with no particular allegiance, who'd come only to witness this player they'd heard and read so much about) and boos, either from the Strawberry Mansion faithful or from proud locals who weren't about to let some kid from Akron, Ohio, feel at home in their gym. Rice, on the other hand, heard nothing but cheers. When the starters took the floor a moment later, the packed house seemed to buzz quietly. Then Mansion won the tip, and the ball came immediately to Rice, who turned to find LeBron James waiting for him. Within seconds, that quiet buzz grew to a roar of anticipation as the crowd got the matchup it wanted on the first possession of the game.

Rice, a stocky guard whose game was straight off the Philly playgrounds, approached from the right wing, his hand-to-hand dribble low and deliberate. LeBron waited, palms up in a defensive crouch. Rice gave up about eight inches of height to his opponent, but he was more than quick enough to make up for that deficiency, against LeBron or anyone else. Now he was going to prove it. The crowd, already on its feet, nearly came out of its shoes as Rice jabbed at LeBron with a cross-over dribble, a guaranteed space-maker that achieved its intended result. With LeBron on his heels and the fans already howling, Rice had the room he needed. He stepped back in rhythm and shot, wide open, from seventeen feet.

Brick.

Maybe, if Maureece Rice had connected on that jumper, things would've been different—after all, a quick shot of confidence and an early lead, no matter how slim, can go a long way. But he didn't, missing on that shot and every other he took in the first two quarters. LeBron responded by swishing an eighteen-foot jumper, forcing a steal and coming back with a one-handed baseline dunk, all in the first two minutes. He followed with a string of look-away assists and a handful of steals, the last leading to a breakaway dunk that had flash-bulbs popping all over the gym. By halftime, the kid who'd entered the game with 2,127 career points, just eighty shy of Wilt Chamberlain's city scoring record, hadn't scored a single point. Meanwhile, LeBron James was on pace for a quadruple-double—he had a modest but effective six points, along with five rebounds, five assists, and five steals—and St. V held a too-easy 36–15 lead.

And it was at halftime that Allen Iverson, as rumored, made his way into the gym, squeezing into a bleacher seat behind the St. V bench. A handful of Philadelphia Eagles were there, too, as were Philly rappers Beanie Sigel and Freeway. A tournament promoter even claimed that Jay-Z, the self-proclaimed "Mike Jordan of rap," had made the trip to see the player many were calling Jordan's heir apparent in person. But since the crowd was already at fire-marshal-taunting capacity, a seat couldn't be found even for a multiplatinum VIP of Jay-Z's status, and rumor has it he never made it inside.

The second half continued as the first had ended, with LeBron and St. V in control, building their lead with smart, solid offense while negating Mansion's game plan with relentless trapping and pressing. Rice, still scoreless going into the final minute of the third quarter despite a crowd that was willing him to score, drilled a three-pointer with forty-five seconds left in the period. Its star player was finally on the board, but Mansion's hopes for getting back into the game were long gone: Going into the fourth, St. V held a 65–25 lead.

Only then did the fans truly get the one-on-one matchup they'd craved. With the outcome a given, St. V eased up on its pressure defense and fell back into a basic man-to-man set, finally allowing Rice the freedom to bring the ball up unimpeded. LeBron, having already claimed the battle on the scoreboard, once again stepped up to take the more personal challenge of defending Rice. This time, the local kid fared a little better.

Rice opened the fourth quarter with another three-pointer from the left side, directly over LeBron's outstretched arm, and it was clear he was finally heating up after three ice-cold quarters. Then came the game's most memorable moment, the one the crowd had been dying for all night. On Mansion's next possession, Rice again came up on the left wing, with that same slow, calculated, court-scraping dribble, LeBron eyeing him from a few feet away. Just as he'd done on the game's opening play, Rice pulled out his trusty crossover— and if the first one was effective, this one was downright nasty. Rice sold it with a hard step forward and a cat-quick pullback; for a split second, it was enough to get LeBron off-balance.

Another split second, and LeBron was off his feet. More correctly, he was on his butt.

With a move that must have had Iverson grinning in his seat, and unquestionably had the rest of the crowd near hysterics, 'Reece Rice shook King James so badly that he fell down. Known as "breaking ankles," it's the ultimate playground triumph, and the fact that Rice pulled it off in a real game, leaving the likely No. 1 NBA draft pick in a heap in front of him, made it that much more impressive. If only he'd made the shot.

Just as he'd done in the first minute of the game, Rice followed up a dazzling ball-handling move with an off-target shot, this time a step-back three-pointer that missed badly. By this point, he had nothing to lose, but it's logical to think Rice might've learned a lesson from LeBron's determined response to nearly being embarrassed earlier in the game. This time, he'd *definitely* been embarrassed, and his comeback was appropriately blunt. Demanding the ball, LeBron dribbled steadily up court, headed straight for Rice. Reaching the three-point arc, he pulled up and fired, a dead-on shot right in Rice's eye.

Swish.

Rice managed a few more baskets down the stretch, finishing with a respectable thirteen points in an eventual 85–47 loss. His twin crossovers were the most noteworthy plays of the night, but it was LeBron who clearly claimed game bragging rights. He finished with twenty-six points, eight boards, seven steals, and six assists, a line that spoke to his impact on every facet of the game. But the stats, as always, told only part of the story—and the real story there, as it had been so many times before and would be almost daily in the months to come, was how LeBron James met the challenge. How he showed more poise and confidence, a higher basketball IQ, and at least as much talent as everyone he ran up against. How he refused to be shown up, and how, when he'd made up his mind about it, losing simply wasn't allowed.

Most people who watched *SportsCenter* that night had no idea that they'd missed the most compelling moments of a big high school game. All they knew was that this James kid sure was good, something that the highlight reel of dunks, steals, no-look passes and fall-away threes only reinforced. But if they'd been at the Palestra that night, they would have seen the whole story—and it would've said even more about LeBron. Whatever Maureece Rice's brief flashes of glory might have done to dim LeBron's shine, the kid from Akron responded, burnishing his rep to an all-new sheen. The things that made LeBron James the most-talked-about high school basketball player ever—and maybe, as many have suggested, the best—go much deeper than anything a highlight reel could hold.

It was only one moment, one night on the arc of an unbelievable high school basketball career, but it proved something to the folks in Philly that night, something many already knew, and more and more would learn as his senior year went on. It showed that while LeBron might occasionally end up on the wrong end of a highlight, he almost always finished on the right side of the score.

Chapter One

Gloria James was hiding. Curled up tight in a metal folding chair, the better to diminish her frame, she sat surrounded by a determined team of publicity and security types whose presence not only kept unwanted visitors out of reach, but effectively kept Gloria James out of sight. You got the impression she wanted it that way.

This was early February, a frigid Saturday afternoon in Trenton, New Jersey, and the woman known to friends as "Glo" was seated at the back of a long, cramped room in the bowels of Sovereign Bank Arena. Directly in front of her stood a two-tiered metal platform supporting nearly a dozen TV cameramen and their gear; before the riser, an overflow crowd of nearly one-hundred-fifty print, radio, and Internet reporters, crammed into rows of chairs and lining the only available aisle. And at the head of the room, staring back at the assembled horde from atop a raised podium, sat the six-foot-eight, 240-pound reason the horde had assembled in the first place.

From her secluded spot in the back of the room, Gloria James peered through the tangle of legs and tripods on the platform in front of her, hoping to get a look at her son. At one point, working for a better view—and with the room's attention focused elsewhere—she rose out of her seat, climbed onto the back of the riser, and stayed for a few moments before settling back into her chair. She'd seen enough, and, as her son's voice continued to spill out of the room's speakers, she smiled.

Back at the podium, stuck behind a microphone answering many of the same questions he'd been answering patiently for the past month, LeBron James wore a smile not unlike his mom's. Seeing this, someone observed that, maybe a little surprisingly, LeBron looked happy—genuinely, honest-to-God happy. Glo overheard, and she smiled again.

"Well," she whispered, "he *should* be happy."

Having just scored fifty-two points to lead his St. Vincent–St. Mary High School team to another lopsided win against another nationally ranked opponent at yet another high-profile tournament, eighteen-year-old LeBron James seemingly had every reason to beam. And yet, given the recent torrent of negative attention he'd endured—a swirl of controversy unheard of in high school sports and made that much nastier by many of the same media facing him now—LeBron might've been excused a trace of bitterness. But if any such trace existed, he didn't show it, gamely answering familiar queries, time and again directing praise and thanks toward his coaches, teammates, family, and friends for their support on and off the basketball court. When the postgame press conference finally ended, he stepped from the podium and toward the door, escorted by his coach, tournament promoters, a few close friends, and a phalanx of personal and arena security. Shielded by her own portion of the James family security/PR detail, Glo quickly followed from the other end of the room.

———

Before it unfolded that night in Trenton, it's safe to say such a scene had never occurred at a high school sporting event. No doubt, there had been prominent athletes and teams that, because of historical achievement or great runs of success, some large-scale controversy or simply the size and passion of their followings, had attracted substantial attention. But before LeBron James, well, everything was just *different,* at least in the high school sports world. The scale of things, it was generally considered, was appropriately small—this was high school, after all. And while there had long been exceptions, of the pitching phenom drafted to the majors straight out of high school, the quarterback prodigy recruited by major colleges as a ninth grader, or more recently the handful of basketball stars who had skipped college and made a successful entry into the NBA, even the best high school athletes were regarded, quite naturally, as largely unworthy of the attention lavished on professional and collegiate stars.

And then came LeBron. And that's exactly when everything changed.

Well, maybe *exactly* isn't the right word, as it's impossible to pick the precise instant that LeBron forever altered the face of high school sports—or even, one could argue, sports period. But anyone looking for a prime example, a definitive moment in LeBron's roughly two-year rise from just another great high school basketball player to one of the biggest and most unprecedented stories in modern sports, would be hard-pressed to find a better set of conditions than those on display that day in Trenton. Everything that has made his ascent so compelling—including the sorts of things that would keep his normally gregarious mother in hiding from the media—was evident on that cold Saturday afternoon.

It all starts with 'Bron himself. In leading his St. V squad

to a 78–52 win over Southern California powerhouse Westchester, LeBron showed off every facet of his frighteningly
complete game: a career-high fifty-two points, including eighteen of his team's first twenty in the game, coming on an
efficient mix of long-range jumpers, determined post-ups, and
awe-inducing dunks; twelve rebounds, putting his long, athletic frame to work inside despite playing most of his minutes
on the perimeter; and five assists, a lower number than he
was capable of but, given how his shot was falling that day
(he hit twenty-one of thirty-four field goal attempts), hardly
subpar. Defensively, he helped hold Westchester star Trevor
Ariza, widely considered one of the best forwards in the nation, to just twelve points. But beyond the numbers, and
maybe even more impressive, were the "intangibles"—those
hard-to-define but undeniable qualities all great athletes pos-
sess. Leadership, timing, and the ability to deliver in the
clutch all fall into this category—and so, in this case, does
the ability to turn a basketball game into a personal statement
of resilience, even defiance. That a high school kid could be
thrust into such a situation helps explain the scope of the
story; that LeBron actually pulled it off helps define just how
good he is.

Because, even for a player and a team so used to sold-out
gyms and TV cameras and highly touted opposition, this
weekend trip to south Jersey was very different for LeBron
and St. V. Just nine days before, LeBron had been ruled in-
eligible by the Ohio High School Athletic Association after he
accepted, without charge, two pricey throwback jerseys from
a Cleveland-area clothing store. The decision, as it was laid
down, meant the previously unbeaten Fighting Irish would
have to forfeit their last victory; it also meant LeBron's remarkable high school basketball career was finished. Only after five days of legal wrangling that saw the authority of a

scholastic governing body temporarily voided by a county court judge — and after a media assault that turned one talented high school athlete's brief lapse of judgment into a nationally broadcast scandal — did LeBron regain his eligibility. Thanks to a judge's temporary restraining order, just three days before his team was scheduled to continue its season at the Prime Time Shootout, LeBron was able to exhale. He would play — he *could* play, as sweet as that must have sounded — and the world would be watching even more closely than it had before.

And so this was the setting: a packed arena, scores of reporters, a foe that shared space with St. V in all the national top twenty-five polls. Nothing new, in other words, except that it was. It was in the air, really, this mix of opinion and emotion and expectation, hanging over the stands and the hardwood floor, and all of it focused on one eighteen-year-old kid. For the crowd of nearly nine thousand, probably 80 percent of whom had bought a ticket for this three-day, forty-eight-team tournament solely to witness LeBron, it was all about the chance to see a celebrity, a prodigy, the next big thing *right now*. For those with pen or laptop or camera in hand, it was a rare chance to capture The Big Story, up close and with perspective. And LeBron? He could have picked any one of a thousand reasons: a championship to chase, a point to make, a moment to claim, cynics to disprove. Maybe he chose them all.

Anyone who watched LeBron James play during his high school career could clearly see that much of his drive came from within. He was not a player who *needed* any external motivation — but when it was offered, he generally seized it with a vengeance. There was little doubt that day in Trenton was one of those occasions, when LeBron seemed to find inspiration in everyone and everything in the building.

More than a little of that inspiration came from the crowd. Surrounded as he was by teammates and security from the moment he entered the gym, it must have looked to some in the arena that he was spooked by all the attention—maybe even scared. And so he made a point to play and shoot and talk and defend so fearlessly as to remove all doubt; and when he signed autographs for a surging throng of (mostly) kids long after the game, at one point sternly ordering, "All the grown-ups back up, or I gotta stop signing," simultaneously looking out for the kids who clamored for his signature and showing the "grown-ups" that he'd neither be cowed by their presence nor easily fall prey to the profit-minded autograph hunting for which many of them were clearly there, he made the point that fear was the farthest thing from his mind.

Maybe they didn't see fear; maybe, they thought, they saw arrogance, an air of superiority in a young man who couldn't possibly be as good as the hype. And so he played as well as a high school basketball player could, with a game unquestionably complete enough to dominate collegiate competition and hold its own, right now, in the pros. As good as the hype? That was probably impossible, but LeBron showed the doubters he was every bit as good as all the scouts and coaches said. And whether he heard the whispers from the stands on that day didn't really matter, because he'd heard them before, so that when he raised his arms and egged on the cheers in the closing minutes of the game, he knew at least some in the crowd were muttering unflattering things about that "cocky" kid down on the court. But he didn't mind if they'd misread his confidence as something less admirable; in a way, he probably preferred it that way. All he knew for sure was that he'd convinced one more full house they'd seen the real thing.

Whom else to impress? There was Ariza, with his scholarship to UCLA already secured, the latest in a lengthy string of very, very good players whose star was dimmed in a head-to-head matchup with LeBron. This was nothing personal, really, not some bitter individual rivalry playing out in the course of a team game. This was simply another great high school baller who couldn't help but try and measure himself against the most-talked-about player in the game, falling short. There was the press, an easy target but an accurate one, on hand to document the moment and — as they'd done throughout the previous few months — making it vastly more substantial by their presence. And there were the shoe company reps, in this case a dozen or so covered head to toe in the Nike Swoosh, lining the baseline near the St. V bench, making their presence known at a tournament of which they were a primary sponsor. In reality, of course, they were there almost exclusively for and because of LeBron, at least as much to impress him as to be impressed. LeBron did his part in a continuing if incidental quest to confirm his earning potential to the world's biggest sneaker companies, who by this time had been wooing him with increasing creativity for the better part of two years. By now, there was more pressure on them to convince LeBron that their shoes, both literally and financially, would be the better fit.

And with that, everyone in the gym that day — short of maybe the janitors, the folks selling overpriced nachos at the concession stands and ten-dollar programs in the hallways, or his own teammates, who'd seen too much of LeBron for too long to really be surprised — had done their part. Motivation provided, challenge accepted, point made. But Le-Bron's answer reached even beyond the walls of the arena. While lawyers worked the proper channels in his name, this was the only personal rebuttal he could offer to those other "grown-ups" back in Ohio, the ones who decided that justice would best be served if his high school career ended immediately, all because a store clerk gave him a couple of free jerseys in exchange for a few pictures and autographs. The statement went out as well to a million other folks he'd never met and never would, who'd formed opinions and made judgments based on what they'd heard or read and decided LeBron James must be a punk, because what did an eighteen-year-old kid need with four-hundred-dollar jerseys or the brand-new, fifty-thousand-dollar-plus Hummer SUV his mother, having secured a bank loan, bought him as a birthday present a month earlier? This was LeBron's response, the strongest and purest he could offer.

Looking back on that day in Trenton, it's hard to say which is more incredible: that such an environment could rise up around a high school basketball player at all, or that, where LeBron was concerned, it had become such a common occurrence. True, there might not have been a day that better encapsulated the swirl of media coverage, financial opportunism, fan interest, and, largely hidden among all the rest, actual appreciation of a jaw-dropping talent. But other days came close, especially during LeBron's final season of high school ball. There was St. V's twenty-point demolition of then-No.-1-ranked Oak Hill Academy, a game played in Cleveland early in LeBron's senior year that drew an ESPN2 crew for a national broadcast and gave the network its best ratings in nearly two years; another nationally televised game three weeks later, at UCLA's famed Pauley Pavilion, that saw St. V beat Mater Dei, yet another Southern California power, while reps from adidas and Nike filled entire rows of seats on the opposing baselines, staring each other down while LeBron performed (and not particularly well, for him) between them; or the lopsided but highly charged matchup at the Palestra, when St. V dominated local favorite Strawberry Mansion in front of a standing-room-only crowd—with Allen Iverson on hand and Jay-Z, who the promoter claimed was literally left out in the cold when room couldn't be found for him and his late-arriving travel party. The sum of these parts, and of a million other inimitable events that occurred around and because of LeBron James, is what makes his story truly remarkable.

In late June, as everyone knew he would be, LeBron was chosen first overall in the 2003 NBA draft, by the Cleveland Cavaliers. This came about a month after LeBron ended much speculation by announcing his chosen sneaker company, signing with Nike for a reported seven-year, ninety million-dollar contract. Such moments are generally seen as a great beginning, and this can be said in LeBron's case; but, befitting his unprecedented saga, the draft was as much an ending as anything, a completion of the often spectacular and occasionally absurd "amateur" career that, thanks to many competing outside forces, was increasingly anything but. For LeBron, the true new beginning would come on the opening night of his rookie NBA season, when the past few years' worth of hype and anticipation could start to be quelled and his game—the reason anyone cared in the first place—could once again speak for itself. Only then could his future really begin.

And how is that future likely to turn out? It's a strange word to use, but given his uncommon ability and everything that's happened so far, LeBron James *should* be a huge success in the NBA. Should, as in "is expected to," but also more subjectively, as in "deserves to." LeBron deserves to succeed because it would be a shame to see such talent wasted, but more so because of the scrutiny he endured to get himself this far. Because, for every critical word written or uttered about him or his family or the people around him, and for every malignant assumption made about the reasons for and rewards of his success, LeBron has only been guilty of two things: saying "yes" on a few occasions when he might have been better off saying "no," and playing basketball with as great a combination of instinct and athleticism and competitiveness and joy as anyone ever has. Yes, LeBron deserves greatness—he's *earned* it, really, in so many ways—and at this point, few will be surprised if he achieves it.

But, on the off chance that future success somehow eludes him, know this: LeBron's story will remain a fascinating one, in some ways even more so. Certainly, that was the logic behind the Naismith Memorial Basketball Hall of Fame's decision in March of his senior year, when the organization charged with honoring the game's history asked LeBron to send his uniform for display. "LeBron has taken high school basketball to a new level," a Hall of Fame curator told the *Cleveland Plain Dealer* at the time. "With the exposure he has gotten and the rumors of him going to the pros and the rumors of the endorsement stuff . . . I mean, those things just don't happen to a high school player every year."

"Any year" might have been a more accurate way to end that sentence. Whether it was rumors that he would challenge the NBA's eligibility rules and declare for the draft after his junior year—or, failing in that challenge, that he'd spend his senior year overseas, paying for play in some foreign league unaffected by the NBA's stringent guidelines—or the pitched battle between adidas and Nike, each ready to offer him a sponsorship deal richer than those of all but a handful of pro athletes in the world, LeBron made even more history off the court than he did on it. And this was no small feat, as his high school career became an increasingly awe-inspiring string of firsts both in and out of uniform.

In the spring of 2001, LeBron James became the first sophomore to earn first-team All-American notice from *USA Today*. The following February, he became the first high school junior to appear on the cover of *Sports Illustrated*. A few weeks later, he won his second straight Ohio Mr. Basketball award as the state's top prep player. That summer, sitting out most of the summer traveling season with a broken wrist, he pulled off the unheard-of trick of attending each of the competing summer all-star camps run by Nike and adidas—playing in neither, but drawing more attention at both camps than any player who did. By December of '02, with his highlights already playing on ESPN, LeBron led St. V to a lopsided defeat of Oak Hill in a game televised nationally, in prime time, by ESPN2—a first for a regular-season high school game. Another national TV game—and another win, this time over perennial prep power Mater Dei—followed in early January. Not long after, the Ohio High School Athletic Association began investigating whether the Humvee that LeBron had received as a birthday gift from his mother somehow compromised his high school eligibility. Four days after he was cleared in that investigation, LeBron was indefinitely suspended by the OHSAA for accepting two free throwback jerseys. When that suspension was temporarily stayed, LeBron returned after missing one game—the first of his four-year career—to lead St. V, by then the top-ranked team in the country, to another statement victory. In mid-March, capping off a week in which the Hall of Fame asked for his jersey and he became the first player in Ohio history to win three straight Mr. Basketball awards, LeBron led the Irish to their third state championship in four seasons. Including the game St. V was forced to forfeit due to the jersey controversy, LeBron finished his four varsity seasons with 101 wins and just six losses. And in the final days of his high school career, he won MVP awards in the McDonald's, Roundball, and Capital Classic All-American games, each of which was played in a nearly sold-out NBA arena. In that, the foreshadowing was too strong to ignore.

That combination of off-court drama and on-court success is entirely without precedent, and it's the melding of the two that makes this tale so distinctive. But the off-court issues wouldn't matter—indeed, most wouldn't have even existed—if not for all the things LeBron has done, and can do, on the court. As stated, the thought of LeBron living up to the hype just isn't feasible, because the hype long ago surpassed any attainable level. But, to its most realistic limit, the excitement is completely justified by LeBron's thoroughly unique skill set: athleticism and body control on a par with Tracy McGrady and Kobe Bryant; court vision, passing instincts, and height reminiscent of Magic Johnson; the prototype physical attributes—long arms, broad shoulders, huge hands, strong legs, and proportional musculature—unequaled by any player who'd previously made the HS-to-NBA jump; and early signs of the innate leadership, competitiveness, and work ethic that defined Magic, Jordan, Bird, and the handful of others who inhabit that most elite group of NBA greats. While straight-up comparisons to any of the above are wildly premature, it's irrefutable that LeBron's proven physical and mental attributes will give him a chance to reach similar heights.

To make the point more clearly: One question heard more

and more over the past two years, asked of those who'd seen him play in person by those who hadn't yet had the chance, was simply, *Is this kid really that good?* The honest answer, so far, remains yes. And if direct predecessors like Kobe, Tracy, and Kevin Garnett are any indication, LeBron James, two months shy of his nineteenth birthday when he plays his first NBA game, will only get better.

Back in Trenton, Glo gave up the security of her perch in the back of the pressroom only when it was time to leave the gym. And that, as much as anything, showed how much things had changed.

Gloria James has been compared by many observers to Ann Iverson, known to friends as "Juicy," mother of Allen and one of the best-known parents of an NBA star in the history of the game. Ann's trademark, especially in the early years of her son's pro career, was a nonstop barrage of reminders of who she was and how proud she was of her son. There were the custom-made "Iverson's Mom" Sixers jerseys she wore to virtually every one of Al's games, the front-row seat behind the basket at Philly's First Union Center, the "That's My Boy #3" signs she held up whenever Allen made a great play (a fairly regular occurrence), and the autographed Ann Iverson trading cards, complete with an inspirational message on the back, that she handed out to fans young and old before Sixers home games.

By LeBron's final high school season, Glo was giving Juicy a run for her money: St. V jerseys with "LeBron's Mom" on the back, a prime seat at every one of 'Bron's games from which to cheer loud and strong—and not only for her son; his teammates got plenty of support, too—throughout the contest; and a handful of cardboard-cutout likenesses of LeBron's smiling face, with tongue depressors pasted onto the back for easy waving. Glo loved it all, loved greeting friends and fans with a hug, loved being recognized, and, most of all, loved seeing her son succeed in front of all these people. But in Trenton? Well, it was probably a good thing she lost her luggage on the trip from Akron. Instead of the usual customized jersey proclaiming her maternal pride, Glo wore a plain white T-shirt. If you'd known where to look for her in the stands, she wasn't hard to find, still cheering enthusiastically during the game; but her usual pre- and postgame rounds of meeting and greeting fans and admirers was largely avoided there. On that day, her profile—completely foreign to her natural disposition—was decidedly low.

Less than a year earlier, Glo sat in a small college gymnasium in midtown Manhattan, watching her son go through the motions of a photo shoot for *SLAM,* the monthly basketball magazine. Asked about the ever-increasing levels of attention focused on her family, she chose her words carefully. "The fans are great. The media—the majority of the media—is pretty considerate. Some of them are pretty inconsiderate. Maybe I should call it . . . very persistent. They can be a little overpersistent sometimes. But all in all, the attention is good. We enjoy it, and we appreciate it, because without the fans, LeBron or anybody else is really nobody. So it's not too stressful. It hasn't been all that hectic."

Maybe not then, but after the TV games, the *SportsCenter* highlights, the Hummer, the jerseys, and everything else over the next ten months, stressful and hectic became an undeniable and constant reality for LeBron, Gloria, and their small, tight circle of family and friends. That explains their recoil in Trenton, from Glo's efforts at self-concealment to the ex-

panded security that made it virtually impossible to get anywhere near LeBron. This, they'd found out, was the downside
of fame.

To their credit, LeBron and everyone close to him have
maintained that it's about the only downside, and that, as
much as anything else, is why he has defied every expectation
of failure. Without exception, the hotter the spotlight has gotten, the more impressively LeBron has performed. Of those
intangibles already mentioned, this ability to rise to the moment is his most defining. That night in Cleveland in the fall
of his senior year, LeBron faced not only a terrific Oak Hill
team, but also a national TV audience tuned in almost solely
to see him perform. His line that night: thirty-one points, thirteen rebounds and six assists. The situation wasn't much different three weeks later in Los Angeles, when the added
presence of Nike founder Phil Knight and adidas grassroots
basketball guru Sonny Vaccaro in their courtside seats didn't
seem to faze him, either: on an off shooting night, he finished
with twenty-one points, nine rebounds, and seven assists
against Mater Dei. Against nearby Mentor High, playing for
the first time since the OHSAA initiated its investigation of
LeBron's new ride—the media-dubbed "Hummergate"—he
scored a career-high fifty. And of course, less than a month
later, in his first game back from his brief suspension for receiving those free jerseys, he upped that career high by two
against Westchester.

In other words, point made, time and time again. *Is this
kid really that good?* By now, there's really no need to ask.

Chapter Two

LeBron James was born December 30, 1984, in Akron, Ohio. His mother, Gloria, was a sixteen-year-old high school student at the time, and while the identity of his biological father has never been firmly established, what's certain is that he was never a part of LeBron's life. Though others have come and gone with varying impact, LeBron's one constant in life has been his mother; from the way he would eventually write her name on his sneakers — Gloria Marie James, one word on each of the three stripes of his adidas Pro Models — to the script "Gloria" tattooed on his biceps and the regular references to her as his "best friend," Bron remains hand-in-glove tight with Glo.

Brought up for the first few years of his life by Gloria and her mother, LeBron experienced an early, tragic twist in his upbringing when his maternal grandmother died. That loss led Gloria and LeBron into a tenuous existence of little familial support, great financial uncertainty, and increasing instability that saw the mother-and-son family unit constantly on the move, usually through the city's roughest neighborhoods. As LeBron once told a reporter from the *Akron Beacon Journal,* there were times when he and his mother were "really scared . . . about what would happen next."

What happened eventually would set LeBron on the path to his current success. During what was probably the most precarious stretch of his young life, LeBron says he missed more than half of the school days in his fourth-grade year. At that point, with a struggling single mother, no steady income, no place he could really call home, and little motivation at school, it would've been awfully easy for LeBron to fall through the proverbial cracks. Instead, as he explained to his hometown newspaper years later, he and Gloria teamed up late in the school year to complete all his missed assignments. Around this time, Gloria gave LeBron a more substantial assist. Realizing he'd be better off with a more stable family environment, she allowed LeBron to move in with the family of Frank Walker.

A local youth football coach and the father of one of LeBron's close friends, Frankie Jr., the senior Walker and his wife, Pam, agreed to take LeBron in during that fourth-grade year. With a home and three kids of their own, the Walkers could provide the steady environment that Gloria wasn't yet able to, and they quickly brought much-needed discipline and consistency into LeBron's life. In addition to being the father figure he never had, Frank Sr. also introduced a nine-year-old LeBron to the game of basketball.

Remembering that day years later, Walker told the *Cleveland Plain Dealer* he saw something in LeBron at that young age that spoke well for his future. "His gift is that you can teach him something, and he catches on real quick," Walker said. "It's a blessing he has."

Busying him with school, sports, and chores around the house, the Walkers got LeBron used to the idea of hard work and responsibility, lessons that paid off in the classroom — LeBron has since said that, after skipping much of fourth grade, he had perfect attendance in fifth grade—and in his after-school endeavors. Already, he was showing signs of advanced ability on the football field, making eye-catching plays as a receiver on Walker's Pee Wee football team. His undeniable knack for doing special things on the basketball court became apparent soon after.

Through those last couple of years of elementary school, LeBron lived with the Walkers, still spent ample time with Glo, began building close friendships with many of his future teammates, and immersed himself in sports. By then, he was showing signs of excellence on both the gridiron and the hardwood, and as he approached junior high, it became more and more obvious that sports might soon be more than just a hobby for LeBron. When that possibility first showed signs of becoming reality, Dru Joyce II was the man guiding LeBron's basketball progress.

An area youth basketball coach whose son, Dru III, was the same age as LeBron, Dru Joyce is a polite, mild-mannered, God-fearing man who soon found himself blessed with an unexpected collection of talent. Having coached his son against LeBron's team in a local rec league tournament a few years ealier, the elder Joyce—often referred to as "Coach Dru," especially when his son was around—couldn't have helped but notice the talented youngster on the opposing squad. Not long after, LeBron was playing alongside the younger Joyce on Coach Dru's AAU team, the Northeast Ohio Shooting Stars. Along with future St. Vincent–St. Mary teammates Sian (pronounced SHE-on) Cotton and Willie McGee, LeBron and Dru gave the Shooting Stars a talented and versatile nucleus. Success, on the local and even national levels, followed quickly.

"They'd been playing together since they were eleven," Coach Dru remembered a few years later, "and every year they were together, they placed in the top ten of the AAU national championship. Except when they were thirteen—they had a big head and they didn't place. But they came back the next year at fourteen, and they actually lost the championship game by two points to a team that had won it four years in a row. So they redeemed themselves."

That success was a group effort, but as the younger Joyce pointed out in a *SLAM* magazine interview a few years later, "LeBron's pretty much always been ahead of everybody. When we were in eighth grade and went down to the AAU nationals, he just dominated."

More important, though none involved could have guessed it, those few years of traveling the country and testing themselves against some of the best twelve-, thirteen-, and fourteen-year-olds in the nation was the ideal rehearsal for what was to come. For a group of Midwestern city kids, those trips to faraway spots like Utah and Florida, featuring games against high-caliber competition in unfamiliar gyms, were enlightening enough. If they'd only known that, a few years later, their high school basketball careers would follow a similar pattern of cross-country travel to play the best teams in the country—and that they themselves would have a chance to be better than all of them.

For Coach Dru, who coached with Sian's father, Lee, the chance to lead his son and a skilled group of young players on such memorable trips was a rare treat, the perfect summer gig for a committed father and coach. His time with the Shooting Stars also gave him something he couldn't have counted on: a courtside seat to watch, and even affect, the development of a basketball prodigy. By the time LeBron James finished his high school career, Dru Joyce II would have spent eight straight years with LeBron, the better part of a decade as both a father figure of sorts, and as a head or assistant coach on his AAU and high school teams. In that time, he's seen LeBron reach remarkable heights; but nothing Bron did, no matter how spectacular, was enough to overshadow his earliest memories of a kid they'd one day call King James.

"LeBron has those kind of things every coach wishes they could take credit for, but you just can't," Coach Dru said. "All I can say is, we kept him busy, kept him out of the streets, showed him what we knew, and they sucked it up like sponges, all four of them.

"And as far as LeBron," he continued, "you could always see that, even as a young kid—and this is one thing I always appreciated about him, from when they were ten years old, when I first started coaching AAU—he never missed a practice. I mean, he always wanted to be in the gym. He's always wanted to learn."

Those words, describing the work ethic and desire of a preteen LeBron James, echo what later coaches and scouts would say about him. They also bode well for his future. Given his natural ability, his physical traits, and his seemingly instinctive feel for the game, LeBron was often assumed not to be a particularly hard worker, simply because, at the high school level, he wouldn't have needed to be. What Coach Dru sees, and has seen since LeBron was a middle schooler, was an enviable combination of innate skill and a willingness to hone that talent. It's a combination every truly great athlete possesses. LeBron, by all accounts, is no exception.

"The thing that kind of separates him is, everything comes so easy, *and* he works at it," Coach Dru said. "I can remember, I used to teach at a holiday camp. LeBron was in sixth grade, and I taught him how to do a jump stop. And the first day, he couldn't get it. He was frustrated. And it was to the point where he was, 'I . . . I don't need to do that. I can just take the ball up. I don't need to do a jump stop.' But by the end of that week, you could see he was going home and practicing on his own. And now you can see the jump stop is one of his best and favorite moves. And it's kind of funny when I think about, way back when . . . not so much that I take pride in it, but I can see how he was willing to work."

Apparently, LeBron James was also willing to listen, and not just to his coach. Of course, the fact that this bit of direction came from someone who shared his coach's name might have had something to do with his receptiveness.

Dru Joyce III, occasionally tagged "Little Dru" both because he's named after his father, and because he's always been the smallest of his group of friends, pulled a lot of weight for a five-foot-two eighth grader. Coming off their string of successful AAU runs, LeBron, Dru, Sian, and Willie were looking ahead confidently to high school. These kids had big plans. They'd already taken to calling themselves "The Fab Four" — a paraphrased reference to Michigan's lauded 1991 "Fab Five" recruiting class, as opposed to that old mop-haired British rock band — and they'd promised each other they'd all attend the same high school. The Akron school district allowed open enrollment within its city limits, meaning the Fab Four would have their choice of virtually any public or private school in town. Given the collective reputation they'd built with their summer exploits, there wasn't a coach in the area who wouldn't have loved to see that quartet join his program in the fall of 1999.

Asked a few years later to name his criteria in the decision, LeBron had said simply, "I cared about going to a school and winning." Asked which member of the Fab Four might have had the most influence on that choice, he was just as blunt: "It was on whoever made the decision first."

It figures that the coach's kid, the point guard of the group, would be the one who made the call. And much as a good point guard surveys the entire floor, analyzing every option before making the decision that leads to a score, the younger Joyce scrutinized the choices offered to him and his friends. One school in particular seemed the obvious pick, a situation literally set up with Dru and the rest of the Fab Four in mind. In the end, maybe it was too obvious—or maybe this coach's son was smarter than his years implied. Whatever the reason, history will show that Dru Joyce III made the right play, if not the obvious one, when he directed his friends to St. Vincent–St. Mary High School. Forgive his father if he didn't really think so at the time. "What happened is, there was a rival high school they were planning on going to," Coach Dru said. "And I was an assistant coach there." The school was Buchtel, a local public high school with a solid basketball program. Dru II had recently been hired as an assistant, and it was generally assumed that the new assistant coach's son and his talented friends would follow their AAU coach to Buchtel. "They wanted to play basketball together," Coach Dru said. "That was their dream, and me being an assistant at Buchtel, I assumed everything was going to happen . . ."

Though he'd later admit to being slightly wounded by his son's decision, Dru II would come to realize the decision was something of a compliment; it implied he had taught his son well. It also worked about better than either of them might've imagined. In choosing St. V, Dru wasn't slighting his father but taking the long-term view on what seemed best for him and his friends. It was, without question, an educated choice.

At the end of his seventh-grade year, Dru began attending a weekly skills session held every Sunday night at the local Jewish Community Center. The open gym was run by Keith Dambrot, a former Division I college coach who'd been hired as head coach at St. V in the summer of 1998. For the previous five years, while he worked full-time as a stockbroker, those Sunday night sessions were the closest Dambrot came to organized basketball. The cause of Dambrot's temporary exile from coaching isn't vital to LeBron's story, but the effect had an irrefutable impact on LeBron's future.

An Akron native who worked his way up the collegiate coaching ranks with impressive quickness, Dambrot had turned successful stints at a handful of small colleges into a dream gig: a DI head coaching job, at mid-major Central Michigan University, when he was just thirty-three years old. During his two years at CMU, he worked hard to improve a struggling program, enduring the frustration inherent in such a job. Sometime during the 1992–93 season, that frustration led Dambrot to a brief but resounding lapse in judgment. Looking for something, anything, to motivate his team after another loss, he got the attention of his players—the majority of whom were black—and asked their permission to use a word he figured would catch their attention. It's not hard to figure out what that word was.

Dambrot, who is white, regularly heard black players use "nigger" around each other as a term of endearment and respect; when he uttered it that day, in was in the hopes of appealing to the toughness and competitiveness their usage implied. Most of the players were receptive to his intent, but at least one of them wasn't. A complaint was filed, and despite the fact that nearly all of his players stepped forward to vouch for him, Dambrot was fired. He lost his job, the lawsuit he filed to try and get it back, and, most damaging, his good name. At thirty-five, his coaching career appeared to be lost for good. "I made a mistake," Dambrot would say years later, neither self-pitying nor defensive as he explained the episode. "It was unprofessional and naive. I didn't mean to hurt any-body, and it was not meant to be derogatory. But it wasn't smart, and I paid a big price for it, and at this point I think I deserve a chance."

He got it, finally, at St. V, but only after five years back in his hometown, during which time he was rejected for open-ings at a few local public high schools, jobs for which he was ludicrously overqualified and would have happily taken. But St. V administrators, who were less likely to encounter a pub-lic backlash over the hiring, were willing to give Dambrot a chance. They're no doubt glad they did. Almost immediately, Dambrot began turning a very good program into a great one. Some of that success came in the form of talent he inherited, some from players who transferred to the school. But much of St. V's success under Dambrot would be credited to the young players who came after his arrival, specifically the in-coming freshman class of 1999. Four of them, close friends all, stood out.

"I had a skills session, where I instructed kids every Sun-day night at the Jewish Center. That's where I could get a gym, basically, and that's where I met these guys," Dambrot recalled. "Little Dru was in my program more than any of the other kids, but LeBron had come by, and Sian and Willie. My first year, without them, we went to the regional finals."

Even before they watched Dambrot lead his first St. V team deep into the playoffs, Dru, LeBron, Sian, and Willie had made up their minds. More correctly, Little Dru had made up his mind, which was all the rest of them needed. He'd felt challenged by Dambrot at those Sunday night sessions, had been playing a few nights a week with high school and college kids at the St. V gym, and saw the opportunity to improve further. And as a hardworking but undersized player who already had his heart set on a Division I basketball scholarship, Dru knew the insights of a college-seasoned coach could prove invaluable. "I just thought Coach Dambrot was a good coach and that I could learn a lot of stuff from him," Dru said a few years later. "That all four of us could."

Undaunted by his father's position at Buchtel, Dru presented his dad with the news in the winter of his eighth-grade year. "He just came to me and said, 'Hey, I don't want to come here next year,'" the elder Joyce recalls. "I said, 'Well, why not? I mean, I'm the assistant coach. Why would you not want to come?' He just didn't feel like he was going to get much better . . . I tried to talk him out of it, honestly, but he said, 'Hey, Dad, I'm serious. I really think I'll grow more playing for Coach Dambrot.' In hindsight, I commend Dru for that decision."

Though he'd left his father in the uncomfortable position of having to tell the Buchtel coach that his own son would be attending a rival school, Dru was confident in his decision. So, too, was LeBron, who'd later say, "I was sure after Dru made his decision. I knew that if Dru decided he was going to St. V, the rest of us would, too." Already, Dambrot knew that was good news. LeBron, a shade over six feet tall when he came through those Sunday night runs as a seventh and eighth grader, was raw and skinny; he was also comfortable and instinctive on the court. As Dambrot quickly figured out, and as Dru II pointed out to him on one of their first meetings, LeBron was already showing signs of his vast potential.

"Keith immediately liked what Little Dru did, 'cause he's

just kind of a hard worker, and he's going to do it exactly as it's shown," the elder Joyce said. "But I told him then, Le-Bron's the player."

With the Fab Four's intentions confirmed, the remaining pieces of St. V's puzzle fell into place over the next few months. Having left Buchtel, Coach Dru began hanging around at St. V practices, in his words, "picking Keith's brain, watching, and then implementing things on my AAU team. Like any coach, I steal ideas." In turn, Dambrot offered the elder Joyce and Lee Cotton spots as assistants, happy to have their basketball knowledge and to help ease the transition for a group of freshman who figured to play an important role the following season. The combined commitments of the Fab Four and two of their fathers to the program caused a minor stir among area basketball coaches and whispers of recruiting floated that spring. Lee Cotton responded in a local paper that spring, saying, "We were going to be around the kids anyway . . . St. V is a good school, and Keith is a great coach. Why wouldn't I want my kids to go here?" And while jealous future opponents may have kept the flames fanned, none of it seemed to bother St. V's players and coaches. Especially not Dambrot, a man who'd certainly been through worse over the past few years. Thankful for a second chance, and buoyed by the support his hometown offered, he was working doubly hard to turn the St. Vincent–St. Mary Fighting Irish into a team that could regularly compete for state and even national championships.

"Whenever I've taken a job," he said. "I've had pretty good goals for the program."

Thinking back a few years later, Dambrot, who'd once said, "I never thought I'd coach again, at any level," described his success at St. V as "redemption." During what would turn out to be a fairly brief stint at the school, he not only attained his goals for the program, but earned another shot at the college ranks as well. He'd had each of those ambitions in mind when he took the St. V job; what he hadn't planned on was the opportunity to guide a future star through his formative years in the game. Asked later to recall his initial opinion of LeBron James, Dambrot paused before answering.

"I knew he was good," the coach said. "But I had no idea."

Chapter Three

In the fall of 1999, as promised, Sian, Willie, and LeBron fell
in line behind Dru, and the Fab Four arrived at St. V, a smallish
Catholic school, with enrollment of about five hundred and a
consistently strong athletic program, that resides on a hill less
than a mile from downtown Akron.

Second-year basketball coach Keith Dambrot was looking
forward to getting his talented freshman quartet on the court
for preseason practice, but the gridiron called first—LeBron
joined some of his friends in going out for the football team
in the fall of '99. And just as he would on the hardwood that
winter, LeBron made an immediate impact with the Irish football team. Though just a gangly fourteen-year-old, he earned
substantial playing time at wide receiver, and by the end of
the season he was one of the best players on a very good
team. In St. V's final game that fall, a 15–14 loss to Wyckliffe
High in the regional semifinals, LeBron caught six passes for
nearly a hundred yards. Speaking to the *Cleveland Plain
Dealer* afterward, the Wyckliffe coach had nothing but praise
for the first-year receiver. "Maverick Carter was a senior and
their main threat, and I remember we did a good job on him,"
the rival coach said. "LeBron ended up being their go-to guy,
and holy smokes, he did a good job of stepping up."

With football over, LeBron turned his attention to basketball. One of many St. V student-athletes who participated in both sports—Maverick Carter, the football star who was also an all-state basketball prospect chief among them—LeBron made the transition with virtually no time off, eager to make the same kind of impression in high-tops that he'd made in cleats that fall. Dambrot, who already had an idea of what he was getting from all those Sunday night sessions, knew immediately he wouldn't be disappointed. "I could tell in practice before his freshman season he had good potential," the coach said. "I already knew he was good, but I knew he was really good when we got him off the football field and he started practicing with us, and I saw how smart he was."

Like his work ethic, that high hoop IQ became a recurring theme in the basketball life of LeBron James—a theme that would both justify the praise he received and help temper the hype. In sports, basketball in particular, the prodigies are often the ones who develop physically earlier than their peers. They're not necessarily that much better than everyone else, they're just better (i.e. bigger, faster, stronger) than everyone else *their age*. That's an effective advantage for a while, of course, but when those prodigies stop developing and their peers finally catch up, that earlier edge often works against them. And in high school basketball, at a level where superior hops and height can go a long way, there's no shortage of young stars who peak at fifteen, sixteen, or seventeen and are never heard from again.

In that, LeBron would be an exception. Unquestionably a terrific athlete even as a high school freshman, he was still a relatively skinny kid. He was tall—six-three or six-four at the time, with long arms, big feet, and huge hands that implied he still had plenty of growing to do—but not so tall that he could dominate simply by his height. Had it only been the physical traits his coaches saw, the size and the agility and the coordination, they would have known LeBron was going to be a great high school athlete, perhaps even a standout in college, and probably nothing more. But when Coach Dru talked about a ten-year-old who never missed practice, who always wanted to learn, who wouldn't rest until he'd learned that jump stop that had frustrated him, he knew there was more to LeBron as a player and a person. And when Keith Dambrot's eyes lit up not because of the height and the skill of this freshman, but because he "saw how smart he was," the coach knew the sort of potential he was dealing with.

With his coaches already anticipating big things from him, and with the Fab Four's collective AAU successes fresh in their minds, it would have been easy for LeBron and his classmates to think they'd be able to come in and dominate the program. Maybe at another school, or in another year, they could have done just that, but this St. V team would have been pretty good without them. Led by Maverick Carter, a high-scoring senior with a Division I scholarship in his future, the Irish basketball team had reached the regional finals of the state playoffs the previous season. That was Dambrot's first cam-paign; with a year under his belt and an influx of young talent, he expected even more from the program in '99–00.

St. V began the season with a win, against Cuyahoga Falls. Playing—and starting—in his first high school game, LeBron James scored fifteen points. Not an earth-shattering debut, perhaps, but a very good one, the game proved an accurate snapshot of what he would do all season: make more than half his shots, hit the glass, handle and distribute the ball. Game after game, the specifics changed slightly, but the final box looked pretty much the same: LeBron would shoot efficiently, score somewhere in the neighborhood of fifteen or twenty points, collect six or seven rebounds, dish out a handful of assists, and the Irish would win. That last and most important statistic—victories—would come to define St. V's season. Whether LeBron scored a season-high twenty-seven points against Benedictine in mid-December, in just his fourth high school game; struggled to eight points against Maple Heights in mid-January, in what would be the only single-digit scoring game of his career; or matched his season high in St. V's regular-season finale against rival Hoban in late February, one thing didn't change: The Irish won.

Heading into the state playoffs, St. V was a perfect 20–0, and LeBron, who averaged almost eighteen points per game, was acting anything but his age. At that point, a cynic who'd watched LeBron's stellar rookie season might have predicted the freshman was overdue for a setback of some sort, and that the playoffs would provide it. The added intensity and consistently higher level of competition figured to knock the kid down a notch or two, to expose him as the child he was. But as he proved, and as he'd boldly do time and again over the next four years, betting against LeBron was almost always a fool's wager. In seven playoff games that March, LeBron averaged nineteen points, seven rebounds, and four assists per game—in other words, he played at least as well, if not a little bit better, with more pressure and against better teams, than he had all season. And when his team needed him to somehow play even better than that, he did. In St. V's final two games, the state semifinals and championship played in Columbus, LeBron averaged twenty-two points and ten rebounds. With Maverick Carter scoring twenty-six points and LeBron adding nineteen. St. V beat Canal Winchester 63–53 in the semis; in the title game the next day, LeBron scored a game-high twenty-five, and Little Dru came off the bench to hit seven of seven three-pointers as the Irish beat Jamestown Greeneview, 73–55, to cap off their perfect season with a state title.

"I thought we could compete for state championships here," Dambrot said afterward. "But I didn't know when, and I didn't know that we would be this good this quick."

He might have said the same about LeBron, whose post-season play earned him tournament MVP and first-team all-state honors. Indeed, many were already calling the then-fifteen-year-old freshman the best player in the state—but he wasn't a household name just yet, as witnessed by the blurb that ran with *USA Today*'s season-ending high school poll, published a few days later: "Defeated Greenview 73–55 for Division III state title. Freshman Labron [sic] James had 25 points, nine rebounds and four assists." *USA Today,* which listed the Irish twenty-first in its year-end national prep poll, would learn how to properly spell and capitalize his name soon enough. But that mistake exemplified how far below the national radar LeBron was at the time—nothing unusual for a freshman but, given how well-known he became in the next few years, almost shocking in retrospect.

The rating and recruiting of school basketball talent is an increasingly national endeavor, meaning players from around the country are compared to each other and ranked accordingly, often before they've come anywhere near each other, let alone actually played on the same court. The process has encouraged (and been encouraged by) the growing trend of top high school teams traveling the country to play in tournaments and showcase games, giving their programs in general, and their top players in particular, both added exposure and the chance to prove themselves against other highly rated players. LeBron would get his fill of that hectic lifestyle soon enough, but as a freshman, he and his St. V teammates kept a comparatively low profile, playing only two games against out-of-state opponents. Neither attracted much attention outside northeast Ohio, and because of that fairly isolated schedule, neither did LeBron. Area college coaches knew about him, of course, with in-state powers Ohio State and Cincinnati already intimating their interest. The small, insular community of Internet recruiting analysts who make their living identifying talent as early as possible were beginning to be aware of the youngster from Akron as well. But beyond the players, coaches, fans, and media who saw him in person that season, few had any idea just how good LeBron James was and might soon be.

And, as Dambrot remembers it, most of those players, coaches, fans, and media didn't really know, either. "As a freshman, he averaged about seventeen, and I said to the writers around here, 'Hey, I'm telling you, he's the best player in the state,'" Dambrot would say a year later. "They looked at me like I was nuts. Then in the state tournament, they started to figure it out."

What the locals were just beginning to deduce, the broader basketball world was about to find out. If that freshman season was LeBron's coming-out party in northeast Ohio, the summer of 2000 would give the nation's hoop insiders and power players their first peek at his burgeoning legend. The general public would have to wait another year.

As his freshman year came to a close, LeBron must have been looking forward to some downtime. From preseason football practice in August through the end of the basketball season in late March, he had been involved in seven months of uninterrupted activity. He got a bit of a break that spring, but soon he'd once again be very, very busy.

To hear Chris Dennis tell it, Akron's basketball reputation was never as strong as it should have been. One day, he decided to do something about it.

A local resident who works in nonprofit youth programs, Dennis is also a diehard basketball fan who runs Akron's annual summer basketball tournament, King of the Court. So it was with a mix of civic pride and the knowledge that he had the connections to make a difference that Dennis set out to promote his city's best young basketball players. He'd known about the Northeast Ohio Shooting Stars since his younger brother played for the team a few years earlier, and as he paid close attention to any hoop-related happenings in the area, he'd heard plenty about LeBron James and his teammates since they first started dominating the AAU ranks as grade schoolers. "The thing was, nobody else really knew who they were," Dennis said. "And that bothered me."

As Dennis remembered it, sometime before the Fab Four made its way to St. V, a woman working on a local historical project contacted him for information on the history of basketball in Akron. He was happy to help, but he wasn't happy with the limited scope of the discussion. "That's the biggest thing with me, that Akron basketball was slept on," Dennis said. "This lady called and asked for information on King of the Court. I'm like, sure, but we've got a team that goes to AAU nationals every year and finishes in the top five—let's give *them* some attention."

Duly motivated, Dennis made an introductory phone call to

Dru Joyce II and pitched his ideas for promoting the local youth basketball scene. With his connections on the college and professional levels, as well as friends on the national AAU circuit, Dennis figured he could help spread the word about Akron's finest. Ideally, his efforts would mean more opportunities for all area players, increasing their chances of gaining exposure and attracting college scholarship offers. But the foundation would come from this current crop of up-and-comers, and, as Dennis quickly realized, from one of them in particular. And so he went to work, quietly at first, putting the word out to friends and associates on the college and AAU scene. We've got some really good kids in Akron, went the pitch, and this one kid, well, he's something special. "There were a couple of people I told about LeBron when he was going into eighth grade, out-of-the-area people, and they were skeptical," Dennis said. "But he had all the little things, the instincts. You knew he was going to be a player. He was that good."

Undaunted by the cynics, Dennis continued to spread his gospel, just as he worked to make sure the players he was hyping were doing everything they could to justify that hype. He encouraged LeBron to play in Cleveland's summer pro-am — a run filled with local college players — prior to his ninth-grade year, anything to get him to face better competition. As he later recalled with a laugh, "LeBron looked at me like I was crazy." Dennis also renewed contact with an old high school acquaintance, Eddie Jackson, a former boyfriend of Gloria James who had maintained a friendship with Glo and was something of a father figure to young LeBron. Finally, not long after the end of LeBron's freshman season, Dennis presented Jackson and Coach Dru with what he called a "game plan" for LeBron's future. That plan, in essence, was "things we needed to do with LeBron . . . to get him involved with the right people."

To Dennis, "the right people" not only meant talented players against whom LeBron could improve his own game, but people within the basketball industry who could help guide every aspect of what seemed more and more likely to be a very promising career. By Dennis's own admission, such a plan might have seemed premature at the time, but it was one of the first steps on LeBron's unprecedented path. Without it, he might have been just as good a basketball player as he became over the next three years, but it's highly unlikely he would have been as well-known—or, eventually, as well paid.

Among the first steps in Dennis's game plan was getting LeBron more exposure on the increasingly influential summer AAU circuit. Hundreds of programs around the country field teams that are either sanctioned by the Amateur Athletic Union or based on the AAU model; many of these programs simply serve the organization's long-standing purpose, providing players from a given city or region with the chance to play structured, competitive basketball outside of their high school season. But increasingly, as athletic shoe companies like adidas and Nike have become more involved in sponsoring these teams, and as stringent NCAA regulations have limited the opportunities college coaches have to evaluate potential recruits during the high school season, the AAU circuit has taken on added significance. The top programs, many of them buoyed by potentially lucrative connections with sneaker companies, college coaches, and even NBA player agents, attract players from around the country to their squads. Such connections can backfire, of course, tainting certain programs with allegations of influence-peddling and making the entire AAU circuit a too-easy target of critics, especially the NCAA. But the players come regardless, all in the hopes that those connections will translate into a better chance at realizing their dreams of playing college and professional basketball.

Despite their Fab-Four-led success on the AAU circuit, the Shooting Stars weren't one of those high-profile programs, which was the reason Chris Dennis was eager for LeBron to spend at least part of the upcoming summer season away from northeast Ohio. Having attended college in California, Dennis was familiar with Oakland's Slam-N-Jam AAU program, and he thought "The Soldiers," as Slam-N-Jam's teams were known, would be a perfect fit for LeBron. Dennis knew and trusted the men who ran the program, and he put in a call to see if the Soldiers could find some room for an incredibly talented fifteen-year-old.

The Soldiers said no thanks.

It wasn't that they didn't believe Dennis — "They respected my opinion," he said, "but they didn't know how good he was." Beyond that, Calvin Andrews, who headed up Slam-N-Jam at the time, said the program was reluctant to take on an out-of-state player for a number of reasons. For starters, there was no shortage of talent in the Bay Area; beyond that, bringing an Ohio player onto a California squad was likely to upset people both inside and outside the program. Local players might have felt slighted that their hometown program was offering space to a kid who lived two thousand miles away, while rival programs might have been tempted to cry "mercenary" upon LeBron's arrival. So it was that Slam-N-Jam politely declined Dennis's offer.

Other AAU programs were considered, but the Soldiers wouldn't get off the hook so easily. With Dambrot, Coach Dru,

and Dennis agreeing that Slam-N-Jam had both the high profile and unsullied reputation they were looking for, the request was put in once again. This time, the Soldiers said yes;
a few weeks later, a small contingent from Akron arrived in
Oakland for an early-summer AAU tournament. For the first
time as a high schooler, LeBron was taking his show on the
road.

It was a short trip, but a memorable one. LeBron played on
Soldiers I, while many of the program's other top players,
including future All-American and fellow sophomore-to-be
Leon Powe, played on Soldiers II. "In the first game, he was
all right," Andrews remembered. "In the next three, he was
phenomenal." With LeBron leading the way, Soldiers I won
three of its four games in the weekend tournament. Away from
home, playing with unfamiliar teammates, LeBron had nonetheless dazzled. Suddenly, a whole new coast knew who he
was.

Finding the right AAU program to showcase LeBron's talent
was only part of Chris Dennis's game plan. Understanding the
influential role adidas and Nike played in high school basketball—each company spends millions annually on its
"grassroots" programs—Dennis had already contacted both.
Or at least, he'd tried. Nike, he said, "wouldn't call me back,"
but adidas proved somewhat more receptive. So it was, about
a week after St. V completed its unbeaten '99–00 season, that
Dennis was in Indianapolis, site of the 2000 NCAA men's Final
Four. The annual climax of the college hoops season, the Final
Four also serves as a massive industry convention for
coaches, sponsors, media, and anyone else with a stake in
the game of basketball, college or otherwise. The shoe com-

panies, adidas and Nike especially, are always well represented, and that year was no exception.

At some point that weekend, Dennis found himself in an adidas hotel suite, where Sonny Vaccaro — the company's head of grassroots basketball and an unqualified legend in the modern, big-money world of high school hoops — a few adidas reps, and a number of adidas-affiliated college coaches were in attendance. Dennis brought with him a handful of information packets; they included copies of newspaper stories on LeBron, as well as a biography he had compiled. He'd also brought a videotape. It featured footage from a regional final game played just a few weeks before, in which St. V beat Villa Angela–St. Joseph to earn a trip to the state semifinals. LeBron's numbers were good but not remarkable that day — he scored eighteen points in St. V's win — but it was his poise, his instincts, and his decision-making that Dennis hoped the rest of the room would notice. He offered no grand introduction, simply popping the tape into the room's VCR and hitting PLAY.

As LeBron's legend grew over the next three years, so would the legend of that videocassette and the footage it contained. The story would be told and retold and, perhaps inevitably, it morphed into something much more dramatic than the truth. Contrary to more exaggerated versions of the tale, LeBron wasn't so jaw-droppingly good that Vaccaro fell out of his chair and those coaches raced each other for the door, vying to be the first to offer this fifteen-year-old a scholarship and a guaranteed starting spot. But he was good, enough so that, as Dennis remembered with a laugh, "Those coaches started picking up those bios I brought and stuffing them in their pockets before anyone else could get 'em."

A consensus of the men in the room that day would reveal

that Vaccaro hardly saw the tape at all, and probably didn't pay all that much attention to what he saw. But the others noticed. Chris Rivers, an adidas grassroots rep who'd skeptically heard Dennis sing LeBron's praises a year before, was one of them. "To see a six-three, six-four kid doing those things, it was just okay, Rivers said. "But to know he was a freshman, and it was in a state tournament game, you had to go, Wow, this kid's pretty good." The best secrets being the hardest to keep, word of this freshman wonder from Ohio slowly but surely spread. More significantly, even as Vaccaro disregarded the tape, other adidas staffers saw enough to know that LeBron was a kid worth keeping an eye on, and perhaps bringing into the fold.

The grassroots departments at companies like adidas and Nike exist to promote the sport—and the companies' products—to, and through, the game's future stars. Simply put, it's good business for these companies to build relationships with and foster loyalty in top young players; if a player is an "adidas kid" or a "Nike kid" at fourteen, it stands to reason he'll be somewhat more likely to go to a college whose shoes and uniforms are provided by that company, just as he'll be more likely to endorse that company's brand if and when he reaches the NBA. And even if that loyalty doesn't hold, those players have still done the companies a service; though they can't receive any actual payment, high school and college basketball stars at many prominent programs are in fact walking endorsements for their affiliated brands, "paid" only through the complimentary gear they receive as members of a team. Many critics—the NCAA and some of college basketball's best-known TV broadcasters chief among them—view this situation as exploitive, essentially accusing the shoe companies of bribing young players with bagsful of shoes and shorts and sweatshirts, then raking in huge profits off the work of such amateur athletes. (To agree, one might have to ignore the apparent hypocrisy of those same "amateurs" generating hundreds of millions of dollars each year for the NCAA and those broadcasters to divvy up.) Regardless, it's capitalism in action, and the best players have every opportunity to cash in.

That summer between his freshman and sophomore years, LeBron James was still technically a neutral party in the sneaker wars. But one company was already making plans to gain his allegiance, and the other wouldn't be far behind. It was still too early for adidas or Nike to know that LeBron would eventually be the target of the most heated, high-stakes battle in the rivals' history. Before too long, that battle would be the worst-kept secret in basketball.

LeBron stayed busy throughout the summer of 2000, returning from his successful trip to Oakland with plenty more basketball to play. Arguably, his most important trip of the summer would be one of the shortest. Pittsburgh, Pennsylvania, just a few hours by car from Akron, is home to the venerable Five-Star Camp. Founded by Howard Garfinkel nearly forty years ago, Five-Star has built and maintained a reputation as the preeminent instructional basketball camp in America. Dozens of prominent college and professional coaches (such as Bob Knight, Rick Pitino, and Chuck Daly) have served as instructors, while Michael Jordan, Grant Hill, Stephon Marbury, and dozens of other current and former NBA stars have come through to show off and improve on their games. Unlike the sneaker company summer camps, which serve primarily as showcases for already-established players, Garf's is less a media event and more a place for players to put in real work on their games. Split into numerous five-day sessions and spread throughout the Pittsburgh area each summer, Five-Star welcomes unpolished youngsters and proven prep stars alike.

That July, Five-Star welcomed LeBron James.

Terry Pluto, the longtime, respected basketball writer and columnist for the *Akron Beacon Journal,* interviewed Garfinkel that fall. With LeBron's reputation growing fast, Pluto wanted an honest take from a neutral evaluator, someone with no stake in and nothing to gain from LeBron's rise. So he called Garf, and, in a column headlined "How Good is LeBron James?" he asked that very question. Garfinkel's response: "I'm afraid to tell you the truth."

Pluto wrote that Garfinkel, having seen other talented young players become complacent, was worried about giving LeBron too much credit too soon. But he couldn't hold back. Having mentioned NBA and college stars like Hill, Marbury, Rasheed Wallace, and Christian Laettner among his camp's alumni, Garf told Pluto, "LeBron played as well or better than any one of them when they were sophomores at my camp . . . he totally dominated. I've never seen anything quite like it." Pluto's column continued with Garfinkel explaining how LeBron, already playing so well against his fellow sophomores, had been asked to move up to compete with the camp's juniors and seniors. Injuries had opened up additional slots among the older kids, and so LeBron was playing in two different age brackets, four games a day. By the end of camp, LeBron had made an indelible impression. He'd also made history, earning a spot on the all-star teams in both age groups. "In the 35 years I've had this camp," Garfinkel told Pluto, "that's never happened before."

There's no shortage of hyperbolic praise in the rating and

scouting of high school basketball players, and phrases like "never seen anything quite like it" are commonly attached to any young player with a decent vertical jump. But these words weren't uttered by some unaccountable Internet-based "expert" who hadn't seen half the players he judged. This came from Howard Garfinkel, as seasoned and hard to impress a critic as one would find — and Garf sounded truly, genuinely *impressed*. A year later, someone turned the question on Terry Pluto: How good do *you* think LeBron James is? The esteemed columnist was direct in his response. "He's the best high school player I've ever seen," Pluto would admit. "I'm very guarded about saying that, because the last thing he needs is more hype. But I have never seen a better one."

As the summer of 2000 came to end, LeBron James's name was on the lips of dozens of influential people, most of whom hadn't heard of him four months earlier. Football season beckoned, with basketball season to follow. Both offered new challenges, and new chances to impress. LeBron would learn to get used to both.

Chapter Four

The combined effect of his freshman season, his West Coast starring turn on the AAU circuit, and his historic performance at Five-Star meant that LeBron entered his sophomore year as something of a known quantity—but only for folks who were really paying attention. He was still far from a household name, unless that household happened to include a college or AAU coach with especially sharp ears.

That fall did bring his first bit of national media attention, though. The various college basketball preseason annuals, published for years by companies like *Athlon* and *The Sporting News* and more recently by ESPN, often feature small supplemental sections on the top high school talent. Those rankings primarily focused on the nation's best seniors, but some attention was paid to underclassmen. And while it's unlikely that anyone at *Athlon* or *The Sporting News* had yet seen him play in person, LeBron was rated highly by both: *Athlon* had him rated as the nation's top sophomore, while *TSN* listed him second in the class of 2003. The word, at least among those who paid attention to these things for a living, was out.

There wasn't much national buzz on LeBron the football player, but area football coaches knew better. Despite the sort of don't-risk-your-meal-ticket specialization that often saw the best high school basketball players passing on other sports— especially football—LeBron was eager to get back out on the field. His coaches, once again, were thrilled to have him. By then standing about six-six, weighing a slender but sturdy two hundred pounds, LeBron was nothing short of awesome on the football field. Lining up as a receiver, he was already drawing comparisons to Minnesota Vikings All-Pro wideout Randy Moss. That season, he caught almost fifty passes for nearly eight hundred yards and fourteen touchdowns, and was named the team's offensive MVP and a first-team all-state pick. And then it was back to the gym.

By the time he began his sophomore season of basketball, LeBron had received hundreds of recruiting letters from college coaches. Many were form letters, but already some were personal notes from big-name coaches at big-name schools; many of those same coaches were already calling Keith Dambrot. They would have called LeBron himself, if that hadn't been prohibited by NCAA rules. This sort of attention was new, of course, and for LeBron, it carried a substantial weight. As an incoming freshman, any expectations LeBron felt had come from within—from himself, or from the St. V program. Now, every one of those letters and phone calls represented someone powerful, someone whose opinions could impact his future. Whatever pressure LeBron put on himself, or felt from his coaches and teammates, he'd shown himself capable of handling. But this . . . this was something different.

So was this: That season, St. V had agreed to play some of its home games at nearby Rhodes Arena, the 5,942-capacity home of the University of Akron's basketball teams. Demand for tickets—from newly proud Irish alumni, curious local fans and, increasingly, college and even NBA scouts—

had far outgrown what St. V's tiny on-campus gym could accommodate. The Irish were simply too big a draw, and not only because they won. They were fun to watch, especially that tall, talented kid with the big smile and No. 23 on his back.

Indeed, there was a great deal more to LeBron's burgeoning popularity than his statistics. From an early age, the kid played like he lived—with personality to spare, something his gregarious mother probably deserved credit for. Ask any of the rest of the Fab Four, and you'd hear stories of a quick-witted practical joker. He's always been quick with a broad smile, which is fitting, considering how many smiles he induced with his play. A flair for clever, needle-threading passes and powerful, gravity-mocking dunks defined his play more and more each season, with the all-important qualification that he rarely went for the dramatic unless it figured to be effective. There isn't a coach at any level who will accept a player showboating at the expense of fundamentals or results, but LeBron's ends almost always justified his dynamic means. With rare exception, his no-look assists and windmill jams drew raves not only because they were so much fun to watch, but because they got the job done. His teammates' ability to catch and convert those passes, along with the aggressive playing style that Dambrot preferred at both ends, meant St. V games were always entertaining.

LeBron and his classmates entered the 2000–01 season with a perfect high school record, and they appeared intent on keeping it that way. LeBron opened with a twenty-three-point effort against a team from Virginia, the first of a half dozen games against out-of-state opponents, part of Dambrot's desire to increase St. V's national profile. The players, who enjoyed the travel and the taste of what college basketball was like, generally loved it. The tougher competition seemed to suit them, too—especially LeBron. He scored thirty-four in the season's second game, and was averaging well over twenty points per game as the Irish rolled to a 9–0 start. By mid-January of their sophomore year, the Fab Four's high school record was 36–0. The player most responsible for that record had just turned sixteen and told anyone who asked that he was six-six and one-half—making him exactly as tall as Michael Jordan. That was hardly a coincidence.

Supremely confident, because they had no reason not to be, the Irish prepped for what figured to be the toughest challenge of their season. On the second Sunday of January, St. V made the short trip to Columbus to face Oak Hill Academy, a prep school powerhouse from Virginia. Year after year, the Warriors' roster featured talented players from around the country, and dozens of Oak Hill alumni had gone on to major colleges and the NBA. The year before, the Warriors had gone 30–2 and finished No. 2 in the country in the final *USA Today* poll. When they arrived in Columbus, they'd already played seventeen games that season. More important, each of those seventeen games had ended in victory, and Oak Hill brought the nation's No. 1 ranking into the contest.

Both Dambrot and his players admitted to loving the college atmosphere their success encouraged, and there was no better example of that than the packed house, outstanding competition, scattered NBA and college scouts, and sizable media contingent present that day in Columbus. Playing in front of nearly ten thousand fans, against a team loaded with high–Division I prospects and a soon-to-be NBA Lottery pick, St. V's talented young players were getting everything they wanted. On this day, though, they'd get just a little more than they could handle.

Given the overall disparity in talent, the Irish probably shouldn't have had a chance. But they showed from the beginning they'd be neither blown away nor intimidated. The game was close throughout, with nearly twenty lead changes and a number of ties. Oak Hill's production came from seven-foot center DeSagana Diop, who would be chosen by the Cleveland Cavaliers with the eighth pick in the NBA draft five months later, and from standout perimeter players Billy Edelin and Rashad Carruth, who were committed to Syracuse and Kentucky respectively. As for the Irish, it was a team effort, no doubt, and they wouldn't have been in the game without it. But with rare exceptions—Dru's five three-pointers in particular—the Irish had a shot to win because LeBron James played out of his mind. He finished with thirty-three points, and if he could have managed thirty-five, St. V would have upset the No. 1 team in the country. Instead, he missed a pair of late free throws in the closing minutes and clanged a twenty-footer at the buzzer, allowing Oak Hill to escape with a 79–78 win.

For St. V, and especially for the Fab Four, who hadn't known defeat in high school, the loss was heartbreaking, of course. But while the perspective probably eluded them at the time, that loss might have said more about how good the Irish were than any of their thirty-six wins over the past fourteen months. To play that well, on a neutral court, against a team laden with such big-time talent, was as strong a statement as they could have made. And then there was LeBron.

Anyone looking to find something in his game to criticize could have pointed to the closing minutes against Oak Hill, when LeBron twice went to the free throw line with a one-and-one opportunity. If he made the first free throw, he'd cut into the lead and get a second shot. Both times, he missed, potentially costing the Irish four points in the process. He could be excused his missed runner in the final seconds—it was a rushed shot, and a tough one at that—but those free throws were glaring. Still, they didn't bother the folks in the building that day enough to overshadow what he did the rest of the game, and the lasting impression left by LeBron had nothing to do with a couple of bricked free throws. As anyone in the gym that day would tell you, LeBron James, even in defeat, was far and away the best player on the floor. His play was bold and aggressive, and he scored at will, outplaying Carruth in their head-to-head matchup and outshining the rest of Oak Hill's star-studded roster. These facts weren't lost on anyone, especially not the players and coaches who saw it firsthand. "I've got to say," Carruth told the media afterward, "he's the best I've ever played against."

Even LeBron seemed to understand the impact of what he'd done. As word of his play against Oak Hill spread, it was clear that no single game had done more to boost his reputation. If anything, the fact that the game was a loss seemed to fan the flames, largely because of whom the loss had come against. Asked about the game a few months later in an interview for *SLAM* magazine, LeBron did nothing to quiet the buzz. "That Oak Hill game put me even more on the map," he said. "The way I played that game, it just felt like, can't nobody stop me. I felt like I got better every game after that." It's hard to believe he *could have* played much better, but the last part of that statement certainly didn't bode well for the remaining teams on St. V's schedule. The Irish finished the regular season with ten straight wins and stood at 19–1 as they prepared to defend their state championship. Three weeks after the Oak Hill game, LeBron scored a career-high forty-one points against Benedictine, and by the playoffs he was averaging twenty-five points, seven rebounds, six assists, and nearly four steals per game. The postseason was much of the same, with LeBron averaging in the mid-twenties, including a pair of thirty-point games, and going for double-digit rebounds on three occasions. After three weeks, the Irish had completed an almost identical sequel of the previous March: seven games, seven wins, and another Division III state championship. Nearly eighteen thousand fans, a sellout crowd at Ohio State's Value City Arena, had turned out to watch St. V's 63–53 victory over Casstown Miami East in the title game.

It was déjà vu for LeBron, as well—he was named both state tournament MVP and first-team all-state for the second consecutive season. But that year there was even more hardware to collect, and those honors carried historic weight. At the end of the season, LeBron became the first sophomore to win Ohio's Mr. Basketball award as the state's top player. Not long after, *USA Today* named him a first-team All-American. No sophomore had previously earned that lofty notice, either. As for all those preseason predictions that placed LeBron at or near the top of his class? They looked prescient, if a little beside the point. By then, there was no real debate about LeBron's place among the nation's best sophomores. In the spring of 2001, the only question was whether he might not already be the best high school basketball player in America, period.

It all added up to one thing: The secret was out. He might not have reached household-name status, but it was clear that he was on his way, and that it would probably come sooner than later. He had the game, the style, the smile, and even the name, a unique moniker that didn't require a surname to distinguish it. There was only one LeBron, a fact that was becoming more apparent every day.

A few FedEx boxes were scattered on the bleachers inside the St. V gym, ignored at first by the dozen or so players in the building. Ten at a time, they were sweating through a ragged afternoon pickup run, subbing occasionally so everybody got some burn. Most of the participants, LeBron included, were current Fighting Irish players, with a handful of recent St. V grads and a few area college players mixed in. It was late May, the dog days of the school year for the St. V kids, and while the buzz from their second consecutive state title had worn off a few weeks earlier, it was far too early to get excited about next year's title defense. Even to a casual observer, it was obvious that many of the kids were going through the motions. That's why the boxes were noteworthy: They held St. V's state championship rings, which at that point looked like the only thing that might pique the lethargic mood in the gym.

From his perch on the bleachers, Keith Dambrot watched with interest, but he refrained from any actual coaching, only occasionally barking out a compliment for a nice play or chiding a defender who'd been beaten by his man. As it was, his attention was split; beside him was a reporter, tape recorder rolling, asking Dambrot to share everything he knew about the life and times of LeBron James. The coach began from the beginning, explaining his own departure from Central Michigan and how it had led him back to his hometown; how he'd run those Sunday night sessions at the Jewish Center, eventually getting to know a precocious quartet of middle schoolers who stuck together and dreamed big hoop dreams; how one of those kids in particular had made an immediate impression with his skills and his smarts; and how all four of them had arrived at St. V less than two years earlier, never knowing how quickly their dreams might come true.

Of LeBron, Dambrot said he'd seen something special right away. He'd already told some in the local media that LeBron had been the best fourteen-year-old he'd ever seen. He couldn't honestly say he saw all *this*—the Mr. Basketball award and first-team All-American notice—coming so soon, but he couldn't say he was all that surprised, either. Recalling his first impression of LeBron, Dambrot said as much, even while acknowledging LeBron's assumed destination. "I knew he had good potential," the coach said, "but I didn't know he was a pro."

He wasn't a pro just yet, of course, but Dambrot's use of the word was hardly presumptuous. Given the success of Kevin Garnett, Kobe Bryant, and Tracy McGrady, all of whom had gone straight from high school to the NBA in the past six years, it was now all but expected that the top high school seniors each year would at least consider skipping college and declaring themselves eligible for the NBA draft. LeBron still had two years before he'd have to worry about that decision; but as he was already considered one of the best prep players in the country, regardless of class, his name was logically part of the "Will he jump?" discussion. Dambrot was as aware of that as anyone, and he made no effort to pretend otherwise. Nor did he shy away, as many coaches might have, from the comparisons that inevitably followed.

In sports, the process of judging up-and-coming stars against established ones is something of an art form, and those who devote their time and attention to the game of basketball practice this art as passionately as anyone. The younger and better the player, the earlier and more fantastical the comparisons come. Fittingly, LeBron James was already being measured against some of the game's all-time greats. Because it was assumed that he wouldn't play a second of college basketball, and because his height and skill set put him into the same general category, LeBron was often compared to Bryant and McGrady—and since he admired both Kobe and T-Mac as players, LeBron didn't seem to mind. But those were the easy and relatively safe ones; more daring appraisals put LeBron up against Magic Johnson (that seemingly innate court sense and vision, point guard skills in a small forward's body) and even, yes, Michael Jordan. The Jordan comparisons, absurd as they were for so many reasons, were logical only in the sense that they conveyed the desire of fans and media to be first on the bandwagon of the "next" great player. LeBron's game was hardly a carbon copy of Jordan's, but being that Michael is the consensus Greatest of All Time—not to mention LeBron's all-time favorite player—the sixteen-year-old sophomore didn't mind at all.

As a coach who had every right to worry about seeing his best player's head blown up to the point of bursting, Dambrot would have been excused if he'd tried to discourage such talk. Only, he didn't. If asked, the coach would even offer a hybrid comparison of his own.

"You know, LeBron's a unique player," Dambrot began, as the topic of the conversation missed a long jumper down on the court. "He's a little bit like Magic Johnson, in that he can really pass. Then he's a little bit like Kobe, *and* he's got some Tracy McGrady in him."

The usual suspects, in other words, and quite a standard to be held to. It was almost enough to make one think Dambrot had been reading too many of LeBron's press clippings, buying into the hype just as he tried to keep his star player from doing the same. Of course, Dambrot knew better, and his explanation, when given a chance, made perfect sense.

First, he entered his plea.

"The hype doesn't bother me," Dambrot began, "because I think he *is* one of the top five players in the country. I know I have my personal biases, but this guy . . . this guy is so talented. He's just a great player."

Then he presented the evidence.

"Most guys that dominate at his age do it athletically, but LeBron has done it with skills *and* knowledge," Dambrot explained. "He's just got great knowledge. He just understands the game. A lot of it's instinct, but the other thing is, he's very bright. So you tell him something—you say, Hey, LeBron, they're running staggered screens, you've gotta jump out. You tell him once, and he understands. In order to get better at this game, you've gotta be able to learn. The guy is amazing from that perspective. And athletically, he keeps getting better, because he's just growing and maturing.

"He gets bigger, stronger, and better almost every month," the coach added. "I think he's about six-seven right now. Well, he hurt his wrist about the third game of the year, and we took him to the doctor, and the doctor said, 'Hey, the good news is, it's not broken. The better news is, his growth plates are open.' He said he could get to six-eight or six-nine. The thing he's got to do is get bigger and strong and tougher, and we've worked really hard this spring. And the thing I like is, he's gotten tougher every year, mentally. The guy likes to win."

It was a compelling case, and if Dambrot was right—if the kid had all the natural ability an athlete could ask for, the basketball acumen of a player ten years his senior, the competitiveness and work ethic to tie it all together, *and* he was still growing—it would be hard to argue with the coach's assessment.

Still, the kid couldn't be flawless. Somewhere in that armor, there had to be a chink, a weakness or tendency that could be exploited. Down on the court, LeBron missed on a drive. A thought presented itself.

What about ego? Or, more accurately, what about selfishness? So maybe the hype and attention wouldn't make him complacent, and he'd be that rare player born with all the tools and the desire to constantly hone them. But if he was really that good, and he and everyone around him knew it, wasn't it inevitable that sooner or later, he might get caught up in his own greatness?

"If your best player's not a hard worker and doesn't share the ball, then it creates issues," Dambrot said, acknowledging the theory. "But LeBron doesn't have a selfish bone in his body. When your best player gets off on passing, that helps. This guy, he'll go through games where it doesn't matter to him how much he scores. As a freshman, he averaged seventeen, and I told the writers around here, Hey, he's the best player in the state. They looked at me like I was nuts. Then in the state tournament, they started to figure it out. This year, he was at about twenty-five a game. He could get a lot more than that, but he's a great passer. He has great instincts.

"Let's hope he's always like that," Dambrot concluded confidently. "He's a fun kid, really. The other kids like him."

Certainly, it didn't hurt that many of LeBron's teammates were also his best friends, kids who respected his talent, but who knew him too well to let him play the star on his own team—even if he was, in fact, the star.

So what was left? Down on the court, as that weary pickup

game continued, LeBron was providing the closest thing to ammunition his cynics could hope to find. Sure, it was a harmless out-of-season scrimmage, but too often in the course of the game, he settled for long jumpers on offense or gave lackluster effort on D, and anyone seeing him for the first time that day would likely have come away unimpressed. Dambrot must have sensed what the reporter sitting next to him was thinking.

"I don't really get on him too much this time of year, but I got on him the other day," the coach said. "Some people were looking at him for the first time—some people that are pretty influential—and I said, Now, they've never seen you play, and you didn't play as good as you can play. And he responded to that. He didn't like it, but the next game, he dominated." Perhaps aware that there was no one more important than a curious magazine writer in the gym on that particular day, LeBron continued without much apparent motivation. At one point, trying to make something happen as he controlled the ball on the wing, he grew visibly frustrated as one of his college-age opponents hassled him relentlessly on defense. At this, Dambrot smiled. "Boy, they're getting after him. That's good for him. He's having a rough day."

Finally, the reporter saw an opening—and since the Michael Jordan comparison was already on the table, it seemed a fair challenge. Stories of Jordan lolling through even the most casual of runs simply didn't exist, and indeed, tales of his relentless tears through off-season games were legendary, as much a testament to his competitiveness as anything he did in the NBA Finals. In such a setting, there was nothing more at stake than pride and his own bitter hatred of losing; what made him truly great was the realization that those things motivated more than any ring or trophy ever could.

And then, here, was LeBron James, looking like he'd rather be home with a PlayStation controller in his hands, or at the mall with his boys, anywhere but another afternoon in the gym. Yes, he was only sixteen, and no, this game didn't mean a thing. But his disinterested performance, coupled with whispers that even during the high school season, he was known to take plays off and cherry-pick on defense, might be proof enough of a deficiency.

Dambrot conceded that it held traces of a valid point.

"It's like, sometimes, he doesn't defend, but he *can* defend. He just rests. And sometimes he doesn't rebound, but he *can* rebound. There's not one thing the guy can't do if he wants to do it," Dambrot said. "And he's got the knowledge to do it. At times he doesn't move well without the ball. But he can. He knows how. He's smart enough.

"Or, for instance, he's a good shooter—he's a little streaky, but I think if he spends a lot of time at it, he'll be a great shooter," the coach continued. "He does everything, he just needs to fine-tune. That's what's going to be hard, and I have to keep pushing him every day. In practice, he'll play against good players, but he's not going to play against a pro, and that's really who he needs to play against. I think AAU served a big purpose for him before, but I don't think that's as important for him as skill development and working out every day. You know, working on his pull-up jumpers, working on his runners, getting in the weight room, working on his ball-handling. Everybody tells him how great he is, and me and Dru are the ones that have to tell him, 'Hey, you've got work to do.' And right now, I think he's 70 percent of where he's going to be."

It was a sign of how ridiculously high the expectations had already grown with LeBron James that such a conversation was being had in the first place. After all, what sixteen-year-old is consistent at anything? Inconsistency is part of the beauty of being a teenager, and if the worst thing anyone could say about him was that LeBron occasionally coasted, drifted, suffered a momentary lapse of focus or otherwise acted his age, well, that wasn't so bad at all. Besides, all any of it really meant was that LeBron wasn't perfect, that he still had something tangible to work toward. He was already great most of the time; next he'd have to learn to be great on every single play. The competitiveness was there, too—in Dambrot's words, LeBron "liked to win." When he loved to win more than just about anything, when he couldn't accept the alternative, then he could think about joining the icons. Until then, he still had goals to reach for. Dambrot seemed confident that the kid would keep reaching until he got what he wanted.

As the discussion continued, Dambrot offered praise for LeBron's support system, especially Gloria. "I love his mother," he said. "She puts her trust in good people." He argued that outside of LeBron, the St. V team was criminally underrated. "I think our team wins a state championship without LeBron," he said. "A lot of people would argue with me, but a lot of our other kids play a lot of roles because LeBron's so good, that they have to take a backseat." And he predicted that, despite passing skills so well suited to the point guard position, LeBron was too good a scorer not to play off guard or small forward at the next level.

And then he tried to guess what that next level would be.

Given the NBA's rookie salary scale at the time, it was a roughly thirteen-million-dollar question, just about what LeBron's first professional contract would be worth if it started in 2003. In Dambrot's mind, there was no question that bypassing college and going straight to the league was a viable option for LeBron. "My job," Dambrot said, "is to make him the best person and the best player I can, and then allow him to have options so he can make decisions that are best for him and his family. If the NBA's the best choice for him, and he's mentally and physically mature, I'll support that. I think it just depends on whether he gets his body and his mind prepared for that lifestyle. That would be my concern."

If LeBron didn't make the jump, instead taking his pick of the best Division I college programs in America, Dambrot hoped he'd do it for the right reasons. He'd want LeBron to go to a school where he'd be able to start immediately because, in his own words, "I think it's going to be a short stop."

The rational follow-up was a question Dambrot had been hearing an awful lot lately. "Do I have to answer that?" the coach laughed when asked what he thought LeBron would be doing in two years. "My guess is that he'll be getting ready for the draft. That's my guess."

One of Dambrot's assistant coaches was asked the same question, and since he'd known LeBron for years, Dru Joyce's opinion probably held even more weight. "Honestly, if I had to guess, and if he grows another couple inches, I'd say he's probably going to be getting ready for the draft," Coach Dru said. "In my heart, though, I'd like him to go to school, even a year or two. You know, I've been to college, I have my degree, and I think that the college experience is something you can't ever replace. I'd just like him to experience that. But hey, will college make him any better? I don't know."

By that time, the game had sufficiently unraveled, and players began drifting toward the bleachers. Gradually, the St. V kids took notice of the FedEx boxes. Impatient for a look at his new jewelry, one of them began digging through the boxes in search of his ring. LeBron was watching.

"Put it back," LeBron snapped in his teammate's direction. Looking up, the teammate snapped right back.

"Why are you worried about my business? This ain't your team."

"Yes it is my team," LeBron spit. "Put it back."

The exchange was a joke, two teenage boys trying to out-macho each other, and Dambrot paid it no mind. But there was truth there, too. In goofing on his big-dog status, LeBron was essentially confirming it. On most high school athletic teams, sophomores don't make such claims, even in jest. But St. V's was no ordinary team, and he was no ordinary soph-omore. This was LeBron James, and this *was* his team. Maybe, as their coach said, they could have won a state champion-ship without him. Hearing that was a nice ego boost; but just the same, they were probably glad they didn't have to try.

The game was over by then, and most of the players looked beat. Still, they were basketball players, gym rats all, and as they milled around, cracking on each other or mulling whether they'd grab a shower before they headed home to eat, a few still lingered on the court, and an impromptu dunk contest broke out. As Dambrot watched, he fielded one final question, this one about how much height LeBron had on his vertical jump.

"Believe it or not, I think it was only like twenty-four inches in the beginning of the summer," the coach said, and "only" was clearly meant to imply that twenty-four inches wasn't all that impressive for a great basketball player. It wasn't a crit-icism, just an observation, but LeBron's ears seemed to be burning regardless. Earlier, Dambrot had told of how LeBron liked to respond when challenged; he hadn't even heard this particular challenge, but he responded anyway. Fifty feet away, as if on cue, LeBron started from one corner of the court, took a few measured strides along the baseline, and left his feet. As he jumped, he cupped the ball with his left hand and switched it—through his legs—to his right, all while still rising toward the basket. And then, at the peak of his leap, he dunked it hard through the rim. It had all happened in one motion, fluid and forceful, and pretty much everyone in the gym had seen it. A similar dunk had helped Vince Carter win the 2000 NBA Slam Dunk Contest, and JR Rider's version—the "East Bay Funk Dunk"—had helped him win the 1994 contest. The other players immediately recognized what they'd seen, and one of the college-age guys put voice to what the others must have already been thinking: "That's it," he spit. "I quit. I'm done." Just that quick, the impromptu dunk-off came to an abrupt end. There was no questioning who had won.

Over dinner an hour later, LeBron sat for an interview with a writer from *SLAM;* it would be his first exposure in a national magazine. He took the outside seat in a cramped, four-person booth at the Diamond Grille, a popular old-school steakhouse located a short walk from the St. V campus; early on a week-day evening in late May, it was quiet and mostly empty. Gloria and Eddie Jackson, whom Glo introduced as "LeBron's dad," sat on the opposite side of the table. After reluctantly order-ing—disappointed that the word *hamburger* didn't appear on the menu, he settled on an entrée of fried shrimp—LeBron picked through a plate of appetizers and matter-of-factly re-counted his basketball history: his AAU exploits; his arrival at St. V and subsequent high school success; his burgeoning local celebrity; and his increasing national reputation. At one point, the waitress approached the table, looked over the patrons for a moment, and finally focused her gaze on LeBron.

"Are you the one I'm asking for an autograph?"

Tall, lanky, unshowered, and still dressed in warm-ups and a pair of adidas sneakers from the pickup session, LeBron certainly seemed to be the only option for such a request. Apparently, two members of the kitchen staff—one of whom turned out to be an acquaintance of Eddie's—had caught sight of LeBron when he came in the door, eventually sending the waitress out to fetch his signature. He was happy to comply, though not visibly flattered, implying he'd already been doing this sort of thing for a while. Taking his time, he inked a pair of paper napkins for the guys in the back. But this was funny—a glimpse at the napkins before the waitress retrieved them showed two very different signatures, so different it was hard to believe they'd just been signed by the same hand. LeBron was called on the disparity. He didn't miss a beat.

"I know—that's *good*," he replied. "That's so somebody can't really forge it. They'll do this one, and then they'll go, 'Oh, wait . . .' So that's good."

The implication drew a laugh from around the table, but LeBron was too cool to smile. Just like other kids his age who, in the case of some unlikely future celebrity status, might absentmindedly practice their signature in the margins of their notebooks, LeBron was still figuring out what his cursive "LeBron James" would look like inked on a basketball, jersey, or magazine cover—or even on a paper napkin. But it was his response, quick and confident and delivered with an implied wink, that said far more about who the kid was.

Earlier in the day, when the reporter arrived at the boxy, hillside building that housed St. V's offices and classrooms,

LeBron had been pulled out of a midday study hall for an introduction. He offered a reserved greeting that implied neither nerves nor cockiness; low-key self-assurance was more like it. Later, hanging at a table in the school's buzzing lunchroom with some of his boys, LeBron's personality started to come out—and what was instantly obvious was that *he* knew that everyone *else* knew exactly who he was. Every kid in that room—whether a friend who said a casual "what's up" in passing or some other student, who eyed him with something like nervous awe—was acutely aware of LeBron's presence. LeBron knew all that, and more important, he seemed comfortable with the idea. Even as a sophomore, he was clearly the big man on the St. V campus, and he was just as clearly aware of his status. Again, cockiness wasn't the giveaway; rather, his easy confidence and sharp but good-natured sense of humor hinted at how comfortable he was.

At one point, a female classmate, whom LeBron obviously knew, approached the table to chat and flirt. He casually returned the attention for a moment, then he interjected—he wanted to introduce his guest. "Hey," he said, gesturing to the white, twentysomething journalist sitting next to him, "I want you to meet my cousin from DC." The girl quickly smelled the joke, but LeBron's straight-faced delivery was smooth enough to keep her from being certain. When she'd left, the guys-only conversation turned to sneakers. The recent resurgence of Nike's old-school staple, the Air Force 1, and the merits of Kobe Bryant's distinctive signature adidas model were among the topics entertained. Quiet for a moment, LeBron scanned the room before pointing toward the feet of a girl a few tables away.

"Oooooh, check those out," he said, nudging his "cousin" to spot a noteworthy pair of shoes. The writer's head turned to find . . . he'd been had. The girl in question wore a pair of shabby, unremarkable sneakers, certainly nothing worth mentioning in a conversation like the one they were having. As that realization dawned, LeBron cracked a wide, satisfied smile.

"Aaaah, we got him." LeBron grinned as his friends laughed at the easy gag. That, evidently, was what LeBron James was all about: a smart kid, clever, and a bit of a smart aleck, but in a way that managed to be endearing, letting everyone—including the target—in on the joke. It wasn't hard to see why he was popular, and it implied that even if he'd been six inches shorter and only a pretty good basketball player, he'd still have been one of the more popular kids in school. As it was, he was the one kids wanted to hang with *and* the one many of the kids wished they could be. That seemed unlikely to change anytime soon.

Back at the Diamond Grille, as the waitress carried the two autographed napkins back to the kitchen, LeBron was asked if he could remember the first time he'd been asked for his signature.

"No."

Did it freak him out at all, especially at such times, when he was a sixteen-year-old giving his autograph to someone twice his age?

"Yeah, it did. It really did," he said. "But I'm used to it now. I got it down pat."

He certainly seemed to—inconsistent handwriting aside—unfazed as he'd been by the request. The conversation rolled on from there, LeBron naming his favorite players (Tracy McGrady and Allen Iverson) but denying he'd patterned his game on them or anyone else: "Not one body—just myself."

And when reminded of his coach's contention that St. V

might have been good enough to win a state championship without him, LeBron was diplomatic—but his answer made it clear that he knew his place on his team. "It seems like I can count on my players just as good as I can count on myself," he began, "and it's good that I've got so much faith in my teammates, that they can score just as good as me when I get them the ball. You know, when you've got so much confidence in your teammates that they can score just as good as you, you've got something there."

Credit given, but with unmistakable emphasis on the facts: They were *his* teammates—"my players," in his own words—and it was his ability to set them up, and his confidence in their talent, that made the team truly great. At casual listen, it might have sounded condescending, at odds with Dambrot's claim that LeBron "doesn't have a selfish bone in his body." But in truth, his statement echoed those made over the years by the likes of Michael Jordan or Shaquille O'Neal, dominant players who didn't mind reminding people that while the contributions of their supporting casts were vital, the stars were the ones who carried the show.

Fittingly, in the next breath, LeBron made it clear how much he valued those teammates. "It seems like we've got a dynasty going, and to start a dynasty, you've gotta have a good relationship with your teammates, on and off the court. I mean, our team, it's not just, we go to school, we go to practice, and then we go home. If someone's in trouble, it doesn't matter, we always going to be there to help them. And we always out together. When you got a good relationship, you've got something special."

As the interview continued through dinner, talk inevitably turned to LeBron's future. He'd already put together a "top five," a list of the colleges whose basketball programs most appealed to him: North Carolina, Michigan State, Ohio State, Cincinnati, and Cal, the last an unlikely choice, except that Dambrot was a close friend of Cal coach Ben Braun. But already, where LeBron was concerned, college was the less interesting topic. The more compelling question was already buzzing in Akron; it was the same his coaches had answered a few hours earlier. Two years from then, would he most likely be getting ready for the NBA draft?

"Yes."

His answer wasn't by any means definitive, as "most likely" was the important qualifier in that question. But there was no denying LeBron had thought about it, nor was there any question he'd heard enough feedback already to know it was a viable option. "But it's not a goal," he clarified. "It's never been my goal to go straight out of high school. My goal is to get to the NBA, and if I can't go straight out of high school, I'm going to get there sooner or later."

There was a logical if whimsical follow-up to what he said, and despite the NBA's standing rule that no player could enter the draft before his high school class had graduated, it had to be asked: "What if, after next season, somebody approached you, and said, 'You'll be a lottery pick right *now*, coming out of your junior year of high school.' What would you say to that?"

"Well, I don't know," LeBron said. "I really *do* know, but I really don't know."

Pressed on the question—could he really imagine leaving high school a year early for the rigors of the NBA—LeBron was ready with another joke. It was the perfect sentiment for a sixteen-year-old sophomore, and his mother couldn't help but laugh.

"I wish I could finish high school right *now,* tell you the truth. But that ain't got nothing to do with playing basketball," he said. "No, I don't know. I have no idea."

A few had already broached the topic, and many more would try in the upcoming months. For the time being, it was enough to know that neither LeBron nor his parents — of which he irrefutably considered Eddie one — had raised any objection to the possibility. It wasn't likely to happen, of course, but it theoretically *could,* and that outside chance would be enough to increase the ever-growing hype. Knowing that LeBron was becoming more famous every day, and that the trend didn't figure to slow anytime soon, Gloria and Eddie were asked if they were bracing themselves for the attention, distractions and unwanted hangers-on who were bound to enter the picture — assuming they hadn't already.

"If they haven't been down from Day One," Glo said, "they can't get on the bandwagon now."

"You've gotta be like that," Eddie concurred.

"Luckily," Glo added with confidence, "with everybody we deal with . . . I don't think we have to worry about that too much."

The family discussed their support network, ranging from the Walkers — LeBron and Frankie Jr. had remained as close as brothers — to the uncles on his mother's side and LeBron's coaches, especially Dambrot and Joyce. They knew LeBron wasn't the sort of kid who gravitated toward trouble, and they were working to keep it that way. They also knew that as more people became aware of LeBron's fame and earning potential, their job would only get more difficult. "We've talked at length with him about it, and with Gloria," Dambrot had said earlier in the day. "There's more people around than ever, let me put it that way. You know, we try to monitor his behavior, who's with him, who he's around, but ultimately, he has to make good decisions."

Secure in the hope that his choices off the court would be as good as the ones he made on it, LeBron's extended family was looking forward to that future. The long-term prospects — fame, wealth, the glory of all-star games and championship rings — were the most intriguing, but Dambrot found himself dwelling on the more immediate future. As he'd said that day from the bleachers of the St. V gym, Dambrot bore the responsibility of helping LeBron be the best player he could be. In the coach's mind, that meant being the best player in America.

"I guess I'm a worrier to begin with," Dambrot said. "But I think he's bright enough, and he knows if he doesn't work at it, somebody's going to catch him. I'll know more at the end of this summer, that's how I judge it."

Chapter Five

The summer between his freshman and sophomore years had done much for LeBron James's game and reputation, but most of the on-court improvement and off-court buildup had been quiet, limited to the eyes and ears of basketball insiders. A year later, in the summer of 2001, the kid would go public.

There was at least one similarity, though—the seeds for the expansion and promotion of all things LeBron were being sown behind the scenes. As he'd done a year earlier, LeBron flew out to California for another brief run with the Slam-N-Jam Soldiers. There was another reason for his trip, though, that not even LeBron was fully aware of. Slam-N-Jam was an adidas-affiliated AAU program, and in addition to the video-tape Chris Dennis had brought to the Final Four a year earlier, the adidas grassroots department had heard great things about LeBron from the Slam-N-Jam coaches. And the connection between the team and the shoe company that sponsored it was tight: Chris Rivers, the adidas rep who'd been in that hotel room in Indianapolis, had previously worked with the Soldiers.

LeBron's potential as a both a terrific player and a prize endorser had already led adidas to offer a sponsorship agreement to St. V; since the beginning of his sophomore season,

LeBron and his Irish teammates had been outfitted by the three-stripes brand. Such a partnership was nothing unusual, as hundreds of high school programs throughout the country had sponsorship deals with shoe companies, predominantly adidas and Nike, through which the companies provided shoes, warm-ups, and gym bags. In return, the companies saw their gear worn by successful, high-profile programs, and, they hoped, fostered loyalty among the players who played for them. In many cases, the deals came about because a program was successful year after year, usually under an established, well-known coach. But on occasion, adidas or Nike might agree to subsidize an entire program in the hopes of aligning itself with a single player. It was no secret which category St. V fell into.

"We all understand the shoe deal," Keith Dambrot said. "It's big business. I know when I was at Central Michigan, I struggled to get shoes. So I know why we have the shoes."

The same logic could have explained the motivation for LeBron's West Coast trip in the early summer of 2001. In addition to another impressive stint with the Soldiers, LeBron, though he hardly knew it going in, was in town for business. That weekend, LeBron and selected members of his "family" — both biological and basketball—were flown to California and generally taken very good care of. Meals and hotel rooms were paid for, transportation was provided, and LeBron James saw just how highly this multibillion-dollar international corporation thought of him. It certainly wouldn't be the last time LeBron and his family enjoyed such lavish attention; but it was, by all accounts, the first. The attention would get much more lavish, and the bill—both for adidas and Nike, and for tournament promoters eager to have LeBron's name boost their ticket sales—would rise exponentially, but the high-stakes pursuit of LeBron James began there. Asked about it two years later, Rivers, who would become the point man on adidas's courtship of LeBron, was candid.

"That weekend, that was the barometer," Rivers said. "How we took care of them set the standard for everything that happened in the next two years."

Arguably the most convincing facet of the adidas pitch—all for a contract LeBron wouldn't even be able to sign for another thirty-six months—was a relatively small touch. Sometime during the weekend, LeBron was handed a new-model adidas shoe; his number and initials were embroidered on the side. It was the sort of personalized treatment certain NBA players were used to, but any high school or even college player who wanted that sort of vanity adornment would have had to grab a Sharpie and write it himself. It wasn't a true signature shoe, designed to his taste and specification, but it was the closest a high school kid had ever come.

"Creating the monster" is how another sneaker industry insider described that weekend; he wasn't talking about LeBron, but rather the process by which companies like adidas and Nike made their appeals. That quickly, the unwritten rules governing grassroots basketball were permanently altered. And while adidas initiated the change, Nike's participation cemented it. As that same anonymous insider pointed out, using a handy basketball analogy, "Nike came full-court after that." For LeBron and his family, the result was that, through no doing of their own, they came to expect such special treatment as the norm. In time, they'd hear criticism for playing along, for trying to capitalize where others already had. The truth, though rarely noted in such criticism, was that they hadn't asked for any of it.

As it was, in the battle for the heart and feet of LeBron James, adidas had jumped to a quick lead; Nike, after a slow start, was in a full sprint to catch up. That left LeBron, who was only beginning to grasp the lengths the two companies would go to on his behalf, to justify the attention. And he did it continually, in his runs with Slam-N-Jam and the Northeast Ohio Shooting Stars, and at the invitation-only USA Basketball Youth Development Festival. Held in Colorado Springs, Colorado, home of the US Olympic Committee, the USA Basketball event was meant as a showcase for the best high school players in the country. It also served to get those players in the USA Basketball pipeline; eventually, the best of them might have a chance to represent their country in the Olympics.

He wasn't yet a high school junior, but LeBron made it clear to the folks who pick the US Olympic basketball team that they'd probably be calling his name soon. Facing some of the best prep players in the nation, many of them a year or two older than he was, LeBron dominated the four-team, round-robin tournament. After a thirty-one-point, nine-rebound performance in his North team's semifinal victory, LeBron offered a typical explanation: "I was just trying to help my team as much as I could. When I get in a rhythm like that, I feel like I can't be stopped." His coach was less reserved in his praise. "I think today showed LeBron James is, if not the best, one of the top five players in the nation, even being a sophomore," said Steve Lansing, a high school coach from Indiana. "He came to play."

A neutral voice went even further. "LeBron James was the most talented player out there by far," veteran recruiting analyst Bob Gibbons told *The Sporting News.* "I don't want to blow too much smoke and distort the kid's thinking, but I saw

Kobe Bryant in the tenth and eleventh grades, and I think this kid is more advanced than Kobe was."

Another city, state, another powerful impression made—by now, it was nothing new for LeBron James. After starring in Colorado, he rejoined the Shooting Stars to play in an adidas-sponsored AAU tournament in Chicago. Antoine Walker, a Chicago native and adidas-endorsee best known as an all-star forward with the Boston Celtics, was in attendance and, according to one reporter who covered the tourney, was openly rooting for LeBron. Shaquille O'Neal, Tracy McGrady, and Allen Iverson would soon join the ranks of NBA stars who showed up to high school events specifically to see LeBron. In the future, they'd be more subtle.

A few weeks later, it was on to New Jersey for adidas's signature summer event, the ABCD Camp. Held in Teaneck, New Jersey, a short drive over the Hudson River from New York City, ABCD had a short but proud history, both as a proving ground for great talent and a coming-out party for budding stars. Banners hung throughout the Fairleigh Dickinson University gym trumpeted some of the former camp MVPs who'd gone on to NBA glory: Stephon Marbury, Tim Thomas, Kobe Bryant, and Tracy McGrady, the last a relative unknown until dazzling scouts and opponents alike during the 1996 camp. LeBron had been invited to ABCD the previous summer, the rare sophomore-to-be to receive such an offer, but he'd turned it down to play with the rest of the Fab Four in the national AAU tournament. This year, though, it was a priority.

Back in May, when he'd sat for that *SLAM* interview, LeBron had agreed to take over the magazine's Basketball Diary. Each year since its inception, *SLAM* had featured a monthly diary, penned by a top high school player, which ran for the duration of the player's senior year. Stephon Marbury had written the first diary, followed by players like Mike Dunleavy Jr., a star at Duke and eventual NBA Lottery pick, and Andre Barrett, who went on to an all–Big East career at Seton Hall. LeBron, who inherited the diary from soon-to-be NBA Lottery pick Eddy Curry, was the first junior to be given the honor.

The *SLAM* issue featuring both that five-page feature and the first installment of his diary came out shortly before LeBron arrived at ABCD. In his initial diary, LeBron revealed his goals for the camp: "Basically, I'm going in trying to be MVP of the whole thing. I don't really feel like I have to prove myself, but if people have any doubts about me, they just gotta come watch me play." As confident as those words would imply, LeBron arrived in Jersey with his family and his high school coach—Dru Joyce. Just as the school year ended, Keith Dambrot had accepted a job as an assistant coach at his alma mater, the University of Akron. A man who'd once said, "I never thought I'd coach again at any level," had finally made his way back to the college game, and while he'd never have chosen the path he took to get there, Dambrot could take pride in knowing he'd played a vital role in LeBron James's career. By his own admission, he'd run St. V like a college team, and that, along with insistence on establishing a tougher schedule and encouraging LeBron to work with and against older, stronger players, played a huge part in the young star's development.

LeBron, like the rest of the Irish players, was initially stung by the news of Dambrot's exit, but he quickly overcame any hurt feelings. Squashing rumors that he would transfer— "Let's say I'm undecided," he wrote, "but I'll probably be back"—and looking forward to continued success at St. V,

LeBron addressed his coach's departure. "I think we'll be alright," he wrote. "I've learned enough that I can help our new coach and kind of be a player-coach on the court."

The new coach turned out to be a familiar one. A first-time head coach on the high school level, Dru Joyce inherited every coach's dream job. It was also, potentially, something of a nightmare. Few coaches were ever blessed with such a collection of proven talent, let alone with a single all-world player. In that, Coach Dru was lucky indeed—except for the expectations that came along with all that talent. All he had to live up to was a two-year record of 53–1 and the knowledge that the best prep player alive was in his lineup. Anything less than perfection figured to be poorly received. Before he ever got a taste of big-time coaching, Joyce would get a front-row seat to the circus that was setting up its tents around his star player. The will-he-skip-his-senior-year question, addressed by the Akron-area media, on a growing number of Internet sites and in the just-published *SLAM* feature, had reached critical mass. By then, there were reporters from *USA Today* and the *New York Times* asking the same question, and while no one affiliated with LeBron or his family had said he was planning on leaving high school early, neither had anyone flatly dismissed the possibility. For many in the media, the lack of a definitive "no" hinted at a very feasible "yes," and that alone was worth a story. Joyce told the *Akron Beacon Journal* that LeBron had every intention of returning to St. V for the next two years, but most of the media didn't get the memo.

The truth was that both LeBron and Gloria had admitted, when asked, that they were entertaining the possibility. For a number of reasons, they eventually backed off the idea, at least partially because they realized such a move would mean a lengthy legal battle with the NBA, which was on record as preferring its players to come college-seasoned and had no intention of loosening its rules to allow a seventeen-year-old junior to enter its draft. But for a growing number of newspapers, magazines, and websites, all that mattered was that the topic had been broached; some wouldn't stop asking until LeBron stepped on the court for the first game of his senior year. It was undoubtedly the hot topic of the 2001 adidas ABCD Camp, and it probably didn't help that, with everyone watching, LeBron went out and played so well.

Placed on the same team as Oakland native Leon Powe, another highly ranked member of the class of 2003 he'd befriended while playing with Slam-N-Jam, LeBron entered camp with big plans and a bigger audience. The camp schedule featured three days of round-robin games, each team playing twice daily. In each of his team's six games, with a substantial crowd watching every time out, LeBron was solid. Well, except for the game that matched up LeBron with the other "best in camp" nominee. In that one, LeBron was sensational.

A six-five senior-to-be, Lenny Cooke was a Brooklyn-bred forward whose game many were already calling NBA-ready. A funny, talkative kid with his own tales of a hard-knock, inner-city upbringing, Cooke had made his mark early in camp—and he was nowhere near a court at the time. ABCD alum Kobe Bryant was in town to do a few interviews and give a motivational speech to the few hundred high school players who hoped to follow his path to the NBA. At the end, Kobe welcomed questions; Cooke's was a grinning but dead-serious challenge.

"When are you gonna play me one-on-one?"

As the assembled campers laughed at Cooke's comic brashness, Kobe put him in his place, reminding him of his

age and promising Cooke he'd get his chance—if and when
he made it to the league. Already a known commodity coming
into camp, Cooke came away from his game of verbal one-on-
one with Kobe more confident than ever. All of which made
his matchup with LeBron that much more compelling. Neither
lacked self-assurance, but LeBron's was of a quieter variety,
at least off the court. Cooke, meanwhile, talked his way
through the week, eventually earning a comparatively low-
profile game against Dhantay Jones, a standout at Rutgers the
year before who had just transferred to Duke; he'd be an all-
ACC selection two years later. With just a handful of people
watching between sessions, Jones accepted Cooke's challenge
and soon regretted it. The high school kid scored at will and
defended with vigor, leaving the Division I college player frustrated and, eventually, handily defeated. He was the player
LeBron James would have to prove himself against if the ABCD
crowd was going to believe the hype.

When their teams finally did face off, it wasn't really close.
Cooke had his moments, including a handful of nifty one-on-
one moves, the sort he'd honed on the NYC playgrounds, that
were good enough to leave LeBron looking momentarily fool-
ish. But those moments were overshadowed by the entirety
of the game, and there was no doubting LeBron's dominance
there. He finished with twenty-four points, including the
game-winning shot, along with his typical stat-sheet-filling
contributions. Lenny Cooke, in large part because of LeBron's
defense, scored just nine. His rep duly inflated, LeBron
prepped for his coronation in the camp's underclass all-star
game, where one final, unlikely matchup awaited.

Each year, ABCD is capped off by a pair of all-star games,
one for underclassmen, the other for seniors. Though the regulations of various state high school governing bodies prevent

the games from being referred to as "all-star" contests, their purpose is undeniable: to showcase the players who've shone throughout the week, the stars of a star-laden camp. Most years, the senior game is the primary draw, pitting two dozen seventeen- and eighteen-year-olds who, after a final year of high school, will most likely be playing at top DI schools or, in a few cases, in the NBA. That year, though, was different, as there was a clear consensus on the two most exciting players in camp—and neither of them was a senior.

A year younger than LeBron and already playing in his second ABCD Camp, Sebastian Telfair couldn't quite match LeBron's hype, but he was closer than anyone else. A prototype New York City point guard, Telfair, aka "Bassy," came from Coney Island equipped with incredible quickness, the ball-handling skills to match most NBA point guards, and a complete lack of fear. Likably cocky in the way great New York guards tend to be, Telfair had years of playground toughening on his side. He also had lineage: His brother, Jamel Thomas, had been all–Big East at Providence and played briefly in the NBA; his better-known cousin was Stephon Marbury. Largely because of that last fact, Telfair had been a known quantity since the seventh grade. In New York, it was even earlier.

A year before, Telfair had pulled off the rare trick of playing—and playing well—at ABCD in the summer after his eighth-grade year. That year, he'd been impressive; this summer, he'd been something close to amazing, and never more so than in the underclass game on the last night of camp. Telfair would later claim that he and LeBron had nearly been put on the same team during camp, but that organizers split them up to keep it fair for the rest of the players. Given how he played on the camp's final night, it wasn't hard to believe him.

Placed on opposite teams for the all-star game, LeBron and Sebastian wasted no time justifying their status as the best and most exciting players in camp. Their showdown didn't quite rate the head-to-head legitimacy of LeBron's battle with Cooke, largely because these players were so physically different. Bassy said he was pushing six feet tall, but five-ten seemed more believable; either way, LeBron dwarfed him in size, and they rarely guarded each other. Regardless of who tried to defend him, Telfair was remarkable. Mixing an on-target perimeter game with virtually unstoppable forays to the basket, he was all but impossible to guard. Given room outside, he'd smoothly pull up and fire, hitting far more often than he missed. When a defender tried to contest his jumper, Telfair used his eye-blink first step to fly right by; once clear, he'd dart into the paint, either finishing on his own or drawing defenders and dropping the ball off to an open teammate. He did whatever he wanted with the ball, usually with flair, throwing in an array of crossovers and no-look passes for good measure. When it was over, the crowd seemed to agree: LeBron had been very, very good—and Bassy had been better. MVP honors went to one player on each team, allowing each of them a claim on the award, but for one night, LeBron had been the second-best player on the floor.

Despite being slightly less amazing than his counterpart in that final game, it had hardly been a wasted trip for LeBron James. He'd played well enough to cement his standing as the best player in his class and, in the minds of many, the best in the country. He'd also shown enough of those NBA-ready intangibles—the court vision, the decision-making, the clutch play—to further fuel the straight-to-the-pros speculation. If that was the downside of meeting expectations, LeBron didn't seem to mind.

LeBron continued his summer "vacation" in Las Vegas, playing with the Northeast Ohio Shooting Stars in the annual adidas-sponsored Big Time Tournament. By then, it had already been a busy, exhausting summer, and with nothing left to prove, he could have justified a long, quiet stretch of relaxation back in Akron. Instead, in early August, LeBron was back in Chicago, but it wasn't another AAU tourney that drew him to the Windy City. Rather, it was Michael Jordan. This, by all appearances, was Nike's "full-court" press in action.

In the late summer of 2001, Michael Jordan's expected comeback—his second, since he'd "retired" twice by that point—was the dominant topic of discussion among basketball fans everywhere. Though by then loyal to the Washington Wizards as a member of the team's front office and, potentially, a future free-agent signee, Jordan still planted his roots in Chicago, the city in which he'd played his entire unparalleled career. It was in Chicago that preparations for his increasingly likely comeback bid took place, a secretive but much-discussed series of very serious, invitation-only pickup games at a semifamous local facility called Hoops the Gym. The invitees included NBA players and recent draftees like Antoine Walker, Juwan Howard, Penny Hardaway, Michael Finley, Ron Artest, Marcus Fizer, and Tyson Chandler—not to mention another reluctantly retired, soon-to-be Hall of Famer in Charles Barkley—there to give Jordan the sort of competition he needed to test himself for NBA readiness. Curiosity ran high among players, media, and fans alike, and the latter two groups were largely blocked from attending. Among the former, those who received invites generally accepted.

LeBron, it turned out, was one of them. As he explained in

his second *SLAM* diary, written shortly after his return from Chicago, he hadn't actually played with Jordan during that trip, but he'd played with other pros, and he'd met and talked with the player generally considered to be the greatest in NBA history. "It was cool," he wrote. "I got to run with a lot of the other NBA guys, and I talked to Jordan a little bit." Of that conversation, LeBron would only say, "He didn't really give me any advice. He just told me to keep my head on straight."

Looking back on his summer as a whole, it seemed that was about all he'd done. "I wish the summer was a little longer," LeBron wrote wearily in his second diary entry. "But I met a lot of people—Michael, Tracy McGrady, and Jay-Z." In addition to some of his basketball idols, LeBron had the chance to meet his favorite rapper, who happened to be in Chicago at the same time. They would run into each other a few more times before LeBron finished high school, and at one of those meetings, Jay promised LeBron he'd come see him play. It would take almost two years, but the superstar rapper would eventually make good on his pledge.

Among the other topics covered in his diary, LeBron added Florida and Duke to his preexisting college list of Michigan State, UNC, Ohio State, Cincinnati, and Cal; of course, there was irony in the idea of expanding his list of potential schools, since the chances of his actually going to college seemed to decrease daily. That was the consensus among the growing number of folks paying attention to LeBron, and he did nothing to discourage it—but he did make an effort to squash the lingering speculation that he'd be spending his senior year of high school anywhere other than at St. V. "It's not going to happen," he wrote. "It really can't happen, and I'm not even going to be pressured about it. People overreacted, but that's what reporters do sometimes. Regardless, I'm gonna stay. I got my three best friends here, and I want to graduate with them."

The other subject on his mind in the dwindling days of August 2001 was the upcoming St. V football season, and whether he'd be a part of it. Common sense seemed to dictate that any kid with a can't-miss basketball future and the financial security it promised would be crazy to risk it on the football field. LeBron understood that, but he couldn't deny what he was: a sixteen-year-old kid for whom a helmet and shoulder pads in the fall felt as natural as a pair of high-tops in the wintertime. Asked about it shortly before the start of his junior year of high school, LeBron didn't bother trying to mask his indecisiveness. "Right now, I'm not playing . . . I don't know, I'm still talking about it. I might," he said. "Every time I go down to practice, I want to play, but . . . probably, no."

If he was certain of anything, it was the chance to appreciate a relatively quiet few days and weeks—maybe even a month or two, if he was lucky—before the madness of basketball season returned. As he wrote in his *SLAM* diary, "Things are just calming down right now, and that's good." If time off was what he was looking for, he might never have it so good again.

Chapter Six

Maybe if he hadn't watched St. V's first football game that fall, hadn't seen his friends and teammates pull off an unexpected early-season victory and celebrated with them afterward on the field, he could have stayed away. But LeBron *had* gone to that game—in truth, he'd worked out with the team occasionally over the summer and even learned the new playbook. So when he finally announced, a week into the season, that he would play football as a junior, the only people surprised were those who didn't know him. As his coach told the *Akron Beacon Journal,* "We always knew it was just a matter of time before he decided to play."

LeBron's decision might have led some to question his sanity, as it was something of a case of heart over mind—or, more correctly, love over logic. The fact is, he loved everything about playing football, from the contact to the camaraderie of playing with close friends and hoop teammates like Sian Cotton, Willie McGee, Romeo Travis, and Brandon Weems. It probably didn't hurt that he was so good at it, nor that, as good as he was, he wasn't the only story. As a junior, he only played offense, and the fact that he lined up as a receiver limited his impact that much more—any wideout is only as good as the quarterback who throws him the ball. He was, without question, an "impact" player, taller than any of the defenders who tried to cover him and at least as athletic. But he wasn't the sole focus, which is exactly what he'd be when basketball season started up again in a few months. And as much as LeBron enjoyed and thrived on the attention and adulation, there had to be something nice about putting on a helmet and getting away from the glare.

As it was, he did plenty to draw attention that fall. At six-seven and weighing over two hundred twenty pounds, LeBron was a prototype wide receiver who had already drawn comparisons to Randy Moss. The Minnesota Vikings' All-Pro wideout was faster than LeBron, but that might have been the only thing Moss had on his counterpart in Akron. Even at seventeen, LeBron was taller, stronger, and by all accounts possessed an equally soft set of hands. Given the comparison, it was hard not to wonder if the six-four Moss, with an extra two or three inches of height, might not have been LeBron a few years before LeBron was—he was an all-state basketball player in West Virginia in the mid-nineties, and he'd played in a few minor-league basketball games early in his NFL career. Now came LeBron, for whom hoops was the no-brainer, and for whom football was a lingering passion. But just because the NBA—with its guaranteed contracts and willingness to turn eighteen-year-olds into instant millionaires—was the safer bet, didn't mean it was the only one. As he proved through the fall of his junior year, racking up catches and yardage and touchdowns, this football thing was more than just a pastime. It was, or at least could have been, his future.

Historically, there's been no shortage of great athletes whose competitiveness and talent in one sport seemed, at least in their own minds, like a perfect fit for another. And while there have been a few who have shown at least glimpses of excellence in (or on) two fields—Bo Jackson and Deion Sanders being the obvious examples—few have actually pulled it off. As Michael Jordan's error-and-strikeout-filled trip through minor-league baseball showed, even the greatest of all time are generally better off keeping their day jobs. As for LeBron, maybe it's too much to judge the gridiron potential of a kid who wouldn't take another serious snap after his junior year. But, based on the opinions of folks who make their living with evaluations like this, it's not far-fetched to think LeBron might have achieved greatness even if he'd never picked up a basketball.

"He had the best hand-to-eye coordination and the best reflexes I'd ever seen," former St. V football coach Jim Meyer once told the *Cleveland Plain Dealer.* "He did things that you can't teach. He just grabbed footballs out of the sky." High praise which, granted, came from one of his own coaches, that assessment might actually be considered modest compared to one made by Tom Lemming. When asked about LeBron after his junior season, Lemming—a longtime, respected recruiting analyst on the national high school football scene—sounded nearly as awestruck as some of his basketball counterparts. LeBron, he said, was one of the top ten receiver prospects he'd seen in twenty years of evaluating prep football talent. "He has the longest arms of any football player I have ever seen. He has huge hands and can out-leap anyone," Lemming told the *Chicago Sun-Times.* "I know basketball is his future, but who knows how far he could go if he concentrated on football?"

LeBron went pretty far as a junior—all the way to the state semifinals. Thanks in part to his gaudy receiving numbers—sixty-two catches and more than twelve hundred yards—the Irish racked up ten wins in the fall of 2001 and made it to

within a game of the state championship. Their season ended
in late November, in a 37–13 loss to unbeaten Licking Valley;
in what would turn out to be his final high school football
game, LeBron caught an eight-yard touchdown pass for one
of two St. V scores. "I was disappointed we didn't win the
states, but for us to go from not making the playoffs last year
to making the state semis, that's great," he wrote in his next
SLAM diary. "No time to relax, though, 'cause that last game
was on a Saturday, and I had to go to basketball practice on
Sunday."

Just like that, LeBron was plunged back into the grind. Outside of St. V's extended football season, it had been a relatively quiet fall. About the only excitement came when he got
his driver's license in late October . . . and a few days later,
when he broke his left index finger in St. V's opening playoff
game. "It was my first break," he penned in his diary. "A lot
of people kind of panicked, but not me. I kind of kept it secret,
didn't let it get out to the public until like a week before
basketball started. It's not really a problem for basketball,
'cause it's my non-shooting hand, and Coach Dru knew I had
a little time to let it heal." As of November 30, that time was
up. Less than a week after playing his last football game,
LeBron would lead the Irish back onto the hardwood in defense of their back-to-back state championships.

There was no shortage of story lines going into St. V's
2001–02 season. There was the schedule, filled with nationally ranked opponents, which a local paper called "arguably
the most demanding of any team in Ohio history." There was
the new coach, who not only inherited that schedule but the
pressure of guiding a team that had lost just once in the
previous two years. Dru Joyce freely admitted that he'd never
planned on being a basketball coach—football was the sport

he'd grown up immersed in—and it was no secret that his only head-coaching experience had come on the AAU circuit, where any deficiencies of leadership or game-planning could usually be made up for with talent. He was blessed with plenty of that, and, humble as he was, he took pride in having paid such close attention to Keith Dambrot over the past two years; he'd taken plenty of notes and learned much about the finer points of the game. Still, he knew what he was in for: intense scrutiny from fans and media who were by now convinced that the best high school player in America was on the St. V roster. For Dru Joyce II, being "Coach Dru" had never carried so much weight.

Mostly, though, there was LeBron, halfway through a near-perfect career on the basketball court, with yet another impression-making summer recently on record. He'd barely played a second of organized basketball in his home state in the past six months—and still, he was all anyone wanted to talk about. Was he already the best player in the country? Was he the best Ohio high schooler ever? Could he lead St. V to three straight state championships? Or, for that matter, four? Or would he be spending his senior year somewhere else—maybe even the NBA? LeBron heard all of it; mostly, he ignored it. "Even though I'm not playing right now, that doesn't stop people from talking," he'd acknowledged in one of his *SLAM* diaries that fall. "With the NBA and people wondering if I'm gonna jump, I think it comes up maybe once a day. But it's okay. Sometimes I like it—I like to hear people say what they think they know but they really don't know."

Those observers needn't have been all that well informed to know that LeBron and his teammates carried some lofty expectations of their own into the '01–02 season. As he made clear in another diary entry, success had spoiled the Irish, and they couldn't imagine anything less. "We're gonna do what we've been doing the past two years," LeBron wrote. "We're 53–1. We gotta keep doing it."

Maybe it was the lingering wear of football season or just opening-night jitters, but LeBron admitted he wasn't sure how the Irish would come out for their season opener against Avon Lake. Turns out he had nothing to worry about, as St. V began the season with an 81–40 blowout. LeBron scored twenty-eight points, grabbed nearly a dozen rebounds, and dazzled the crowd with an array of assists, dunks, and blocked shots. As they would in virtually all their home games that season, the Irish played in front of a big crowd at Rhodes Arena, the gym at nearby Akron U. They'd picked up where they'd left off seven months earlier, and they'd made it look easy. It would be one of the few times "easy" applied to their schedule all season.

The next day, December 1, St. V played the first of a half dozen games that season against nationally ranked opponents. Their initial test came against Germantown Academy, a Philadelphia-area private school with three players who were considered among the top hundred seniors in the country. The best of them was Matt Walsh, a six-six wing who'd already committed to the University of Florida and figured to match up with LeBron. And while it was impossible, so early in the season and with two teams that had never faced each other, to guess how evenly matched the teams might be, the game looked awfully close on paper: Coming in, Germantown was ranked fifth in *USA Today*'s national high school poll, one spot ahead of the Irish. "I love games like this," LeBron wrote in his diary at the time. "You get 5,600 people coming to your game. Playing good teams, in big games like that, that's what it's all about."

As expected, St. V's second game was much closer than its first, but it had two important things in common: the Irish won, and LeBron was virtually unstoppable, scoring thirty-eight points and adding sixteen rebounds in a 70–64 victory. Walsh led Germantown with twenty-four, but it was St. V, playing in front of another large, expectant crowd at Rhodes Arena, that successfully defended its place among the nation's best high school teams. And it was LeBron, as usual, who had the most to do with that success—so it wasn't surprising that, after the game, yet another opposing coach added to LeBron's growing list of hard-to-believe accolades. This one wasn't original, but it was nonetheless compelling. "LeBron is the best player we've ever played against," said Germantown coach Jim Fenerty, who a few years earlier had coached his team against a Lower Merion (PA) High School team that featured a precocious, do-everything guard named Kobe Bryant. "Right now, he's a better overall player than Kobe was as a senior."

If it wasn't already, the Kobe comparison would soon become the most popular among those looking to link LeBron to a current NBA star. And that comparison worked, mostly, for a number of obvious reasons. Both had the height to play either shooting guard or small forward, with the ball-handling and passing skills to help out at the point. Neither was a natural-born shooter, but both had shown a knack for hitting jumpers when they mattered most. But the reason the comparison existed at all—and why Tracy McGrady's name would come up nearly as often—was because of how Kobe came into the league. He'd skipped college, and by then, pretty much everyone assumed LeBron would do the same.

What made the Kobe references so interesting were the comparisons not to the current Kobe, the NBA all-star who most agreed was one of the top five players in the league, but to Kobe "at the same age." In that, the consensus was clear: LeBron the high school junior was better—maybe even much better—than Kobe had been at the same age. Most who'd seen both players as high schoolers agreed that LeBron was physically stronger, and a better ball handler and passer, than Kobe had been seven years earlier. No doubt, that favorable comparison spoke to how ahead-of-his-time good LeBron already was, but it also, if more quietly, revealed how Kobe's example allowed LeBron to garner so much attention. By turning out so well, players like Kobe, McGrady, Jermaine O'Neal, and Kevin Garnett—the latter ranking as the originator of the end-of-the-century trend of high school stars coming directly into the NBA—changed the way their successors would be viewed. Today, instead of wondering if top prep players might *consider* skipping college, most people assume that at least a few of the best players each year will enter the draft. Taken a step further, this new reality means there's increased attention not only on high school seniors, but on juniors, sophomores, freshmen, and even a handful of junior high kids as fans, scouts, and media try to spot the next round of players good enough to ignore college.

For LeBron James, who by the end of his freshman season was the best player on an unbeaten, state-championship-winning team, the attention would have come regardless. But it probably wouldn't have come as early, or with anything like the intensity, if not for the triumphant leaps made by his predecessors. Now all LeBron had to do was justify it every time he took the court, something St. V's schedule made an ongoing challenge.

After their back-to-back wins to open the season, the Irish enjoyed a week between games before welcoming another highly rated opponent. Vashon High School, a perennial power from St. Louis, arrived in Akron with the nation's No. 7 ranking according to *USA Today*. Their star was Jimmy McKinney, a six-four senior who'd committed to play at the University of Missouri and was considered one of the best shooting guards in the country. Like St. V, Vashon was a defending state champ led by a stellar individual talent; fittingly, they guarded each other when the teams met up at Rhodes Arena. Hoping to keep the game low-scoring and limit LeBron's output, Vashon slowed the game's pace. The strategy was somewhat successful, as neither team reached the fifty-point mark. It also helped keep one of the game's stars from a typically bloated stat line — McKinney, a terrific scorer, was held to nine points. He fouled out in the closing minutes of the game.

LeBron, meanwhile, scored twenty-six points and hauled in nine boards as St. V came away with a 49–41 win. Those twenty-six points ranked as his lowest point total of the young season; it was also the second straight game in which he accounted for more than half his team's points. In other words, LeBron was at least meeting every expectation, and probably surpassing all but the most unrealistic. Just ten days into their season, the Irish had already beaten two of the best teams in America, and nothing — not a coaching change, their grueling schedule, or the long-running football season that had held up most of their best players — seemed able to slow them down. "Now people are wondering if we're the best team in the country," LeBron wrote in his next *SLAM* diary. "I can't say that, but I think we're up there — we *are* up there. We ain't got four All-Americans, but we got great role players, and we play defense. And when it's game time, we definitely come to play."

It was hard to argue, especially when LeBron acknowledged his teammates. "Role players" might have seemed demeaning to some, but the fact was that aside from LeBron, St. V was blessed with a group of talented players, none stars in their own right but a half dozen of them good enough to play on almost any high school team in the nation. The rest of the Fab Four—Lil' Dru, Sian, and Willie—formed the core of that supporting cast, while fellow junior Romeo Travis, sophomores Brandon Weems and and Corey Jones, and seniors Sekou Lewis and Chad Mraz also played key roles. Together, they gave Coach Dru shooters, ball handlers, defenders, and rebounders, a varied mix of height and speed and strength and scoring that could be mixed and matched to handle almost any matchup. And in LeBron, not just a great player but one who excelled at that almost magical basketball skill of "making the players around him better," they had the perfect foundation on which to build. Just as important, the Irish owned a rare and—judging by the results—nearly perfect blend of personalities, of high school kids whose attitudes and work ethic fit so well with their coach and each other. "When you see our team play, you recognize, we're not the most athletic, we're not the most talented, but they win because they play so smart," Coach Dru had said before the start of the season. "All that time playing together, they know each other in and out, and they challenge one another to be better. They don't accept any half-stepping or taking a day off. They're pushing one another all the time. When you get a cohesiveness that's already built in, it just takes it to the next level."

With seemingly everything going for it, St. V rolled toward the new year with a string of quality wins. A week after beating Vashon, the Irish hosted Louisville's Male High School, yet another team that had opened the season in the *USA Today* Top 25. LeBron totaled thirty-seven points and filled the rest of the stat sheet as St. V upended Male, 90–69. A week later, in a game one local paper called a possible state-final preview, the Irish needed a late run and twenty-nine points from LeBron to beat Cincinnati's Roger Bacon HS, 79–70; the next day, showing no signs of wear in his second game of the weekend, LeBron posted a line that was nothing short of remarkable. Facing Detroit's Redford High at Rhodes Arena—a solid team led by talented junior Dion Harris—LeBron totaled forty-three points, a career high, along with nine rebounds and eight assists. Neither fifty-point games nor triple-doubles are all that common on any level of basketball, and LeBron came close to both in the same game. As it was, the Irish needed all of his contributions in an 81–78 win.

After a few days off around Christmas, St. V made its first road trip of the season, arriving in Delaware for the annual Slam Dunk to the Beach tournament, one of the oldest and biggest of a growing number of nationally attended high school hoop tournaments. The Irish opened against St. Benedict of New Jersey, and while they gave up more points and committed more turnovers than their coach would have liked, they held on for a 67–60 victory. LeBron, apparently playing through a touch of the flu, had his worst game of the year, scoring just eighteen points. Two nights later, against Amityville High of Long Island, NY, the Irish once again gave up too many points, continuing one unsettling trend and ending another one—their winning streak. Led by twenty-eight points and eighteen rebounds from All-American center Jason Fraser, Amityville overcame thirty-nine points from LeBron for an 84–83 win. The first loss of his junior year came on his seventeenth birthday; he completed a four-point play in the final ten seconds, then just missed a last-second jumper from well beyond the NBA three-point line that would have won the game. But he didn't, and St. V entered 2002 with a loss.

"Basically, we played good and they played great," LeBron wrote in his next diary. "To tell you the truth, though, I think it made us better. It told us that we can be beat, that we have to turn up our intensity."

Duly motivated, St. V returned home and strolled through January against largely inferior local competition, going 7–0 in the month. It was a quiet run, mostly, except for one game in mid-January in which, as LeBron recalled in his next *SLAM* diary, "I took more hits than I did the whole football season." The opponent was Brush High School, and like most of St. V's in-state opponents, Brush never had a chance. The ensuing frustration of being on the wrong end of a blowout—in this case a 71–46 Irish victory—showed itself in physical play and trash talking throughout the contest. Eventually, it manifested itself in the form of a cheap shot against the biggest target on the floor.

Roy Hall was one of Brush's top basketball players; he was even better in football, an all-state pick who was headed to Ohio State on a scholarship in the fall. On this night, though, stymied by LeBron and the St. V defense, he chose an unfortunate time to showcase his gridiron prowess. Late in the game, with the outcome already decided, Hall was stripped of the ball by LeBron, who took off for what figured to be an uncontested dunk. Hall gave chase and—as LeBron prepared to take off—tackled him. LeBron was unhurt, and after a brief bit of shouting and posturing, the teams relaxed, and Hall and LeBron eventually exchanged a handshake and a quick hug.

Despite the cordial ending, the game was a lesson to the

Irish, and especially their best player, on the price to be paid for their dominance. "They were trying to punk us the whole night, so we had to get in their heads," LeBron explained in his diary. "Them trying to get into it physical with us, we had to get into them mentally."

Beyond that brief disturbance, the Irish continued to cruise through the regular season. And their wins were largely consistent: LeBron was amazing, two or three or four of his teammates played their roles to perfection beside him, and St. V's aggressive-at-both-ends style put teams away early. At their best, the Irish were no fun to play against but a joy to watch, a credit to the players and to both Dambrot and Coach Dru, the coaches who'd started and maintained the program's high standards. Any team so steadily successful figured to draw more attention, something the daily coverage in the Akron and Cleveland papers and the crowds of five-thousand-plus at Rhodes Arena made obvious. But there was much more to all this interest in St. V than simply the appeal of a successful high school program. The attention, a mounting drone that seemed to grow louder by the day, existed almost solely because of LeBron. Stories in the local papers were expected; pieces in the *New York Times* and *Daily News,* along with an Associated Press profile that ran in dozens of papers around the country, were something different. The swirl of coverage that first blew up around LeBron in the summer of 2001, only to settle briefly in the fall, had kicked back up with a force. It was about to become a full-blown storm.

Chapter Seven

St. V began February the same way it had ended January—
with a blowout win over a local rival. Seven days after they
hammered Buchtel, the school where LeBron and the rest of
the Fab Four had appeared destined to end up only a few
years earlier, the Irish dominated Archbishop Hoban. LeBron
topped thirty points in both games, and St. V stood at 15–1
going into its biggest game of the year. The opponent, as it
had been thirteen months earlier, was Oak Hill Academy.

The stakes of the matchup had been lowered ever so
slightly a week earlier, when Oak Hill suffered its first loss in
two years and dropped from the No. 1 spot in the *USA Today*
national rankings. But the Warriors hadn't dropped far—both
teams entered the game with top-five rankings—and the rivalry that had developed after their first meeting had sim-
mered to a boil as the rematch approached. Longtime Oak Hill
coach Steve Smith had apparently slighted the St. V players—
LeBron excepted, of course—after the 2001 game, allegedly
referring to the Irish as a "JV squad." Their neck-and-neck poll
position and one-loss-apiece records only added to the
drama. But the real selling point of this game, the thing that
would draw NBA execs and a bigger-than-ever media horde
to a neutral-site game, was the one-on-one battle between

LeBron and Oak Hill senior forward Carmelo Anthony. Without any of the hype of his younger counterpart, Anthony was having a terrific year, and by the time of their mid-February meeting, he was arguably the only player in America whose all-around talent was seen as comparable to LeBron's.

As with so much else in LeBron's rise, timing played a key role in making the game as big as it was. The venue was the Sovereign Bank Arena in Trenton, New Jersey, home of the annual Prime Time Shootout. Like the Slam Dunk to the Beach tourney at which the Irish had suffered their first loss a month and a half earlier, the Prime Time was a multiday invitational showcase for prominent teams from around the country; unlike Slam Dunk, which ran a tournament format where teams advanced through brackets toward a championship, the Prime Time was a one-and-done affair. For each of the few dozen teams that participated, there were no titles or trophies to claim, only bragging rights against another very good team. The bigger prize, potentially, went to the tournament promoters, for whom the presence of nationally prominent teams with well-known players could mean a nice payday. The number of such events seemed to double every winter, and many of them were purely profit-driven; notably, proceeds from the Prime Time—which had quickly established itself as one of the top events of its kind in the county—went to a local charitable group. Maybe it was karma, then, that gave the Prime Time's organizers such perfect timing.

As marketable matchups went, both between teams and individual players, the St. V–Oak Hill game couldn't have been topped in the winter of 2002. Nor could the location: While the Prime Time was settled in Trenton, it had received an unexpected gift when the 2002 NBA All-Star Game was awarded to Philly, less than an hour's drive from Trenton. The

NBA's annual midseason showcase was held at a different site each year; its placement that year, so close to Trenton, meant a sizable array of basketball power brokers—players, scouts, media, and team and league executives—were close enough to swing by for a look. The scheduling couldn't have been better, either: the Irish and Warriors were scheduled to tip off early Sunday afternoon, while the All-Star Game was set for midevening, giving anyone hoping to attend both just enough time to make it. In St. V–Oak Hill, they had a game worth looking at; in LeBron and Carmelo, they had two players many expected to see in All-Star games of their own in the next few years. And in LeBron especially, they had something unusual, even unprecedented, to talk about. As they'd all know soon enough, this was the kid who was going to be on the next cover of *Sports Illustrated*.

A hot rumor, whispered by a few in-the-know folks that day in Trenton, it would be confirmed as fact in the next few days: LeBron James would be one of only a handful of high school athletes ever—and the first underclass basketball player—to grace the front of the most respected and widely read sports magazine in the world. That was big, and while the game itself didn't really need any additional hype, news of LeBron's *SI* cover would, especially in hindsight, make the weekend one of the most memorable of LeBron's high school career. Of course, the game had something to do with it, too. A day earlier, in his annual All-Star weekend press conference, NBA commissioner David Stern had fielded a number of questions about LeBron and rumors that he might test the NBA's draft-eligibility rules by leaving high school a year early. On Sunday, LeBron showed why the idea might not have been so crazy.

Considering how close the previous year's game had been,

how St. V's core group of players was a year older, bigger, and more experienced, and how many players Oak Hill had lost to graduation from its unbeaten 2000–01 team, it wasn't hard to imagine that the Irish had the advantage in their rematch. But the Warriors, with as many as eight Division I prospects on their roster, immediately showed that their 25–1 record coming into the game was no fluke. Owning a substantial size advantage in the frontcourt, Oak Hill dominated in the paint; the Irish, meanwhile, struggled to hit shots—except for LeBron. Wearing a pair of American-flag-patterned, Kobe-Bryant-model adidas high-tops—given with Bryant's blessing—he was, as usual, essentially unstoppable, scoring from near and far, rebounding aggressively, passing with flair. Even with many of his teammates having subpar games, LeBron's excellence might have been enough against most teams. Oak Hill, though, was anything but, and unlike almost every other team in the country, they had a player who might have been just as good as LeBron James.

When it was over, it was hard to argue that LeBron James had been the best player on the floor. Unfortunately for the Irish, Carmelo had been nearly as good, and—as hard as the rest of the St. V kids worked—he had a great deal more talent around him. Down by double digits early, the Irish had battled back and stayed close throughout the second half, only to fall in the end, 72–66. LeBron finished with thirty-six points, Carmelo thirty-four. Friends from their time at the USA Basketball Youth Development Festival the previous summer, both had shown remarkably complete games, confirming the thought shared by many—that the two best high school players in America might have been on the same floor that day. Starring for Syracuse a little more than a year later, Carmelo would be the best player on the floor in the 2003 NCAA championship game; LeBron would be watching and cheering him on. For the time being, it was left to Smith, the Oak Hill coach, to put both players' talents in perspective.

"Carmelo is probably one of the top five players I've ever coached," said Smith, who counted Jerry Stackhouse, Ron Mercer, Stephen Jackson, and numerous other NBA players among his Oak Hill alumni. "And there's no question that LeBron is the best player I've ever coached against."

That was a matter of opinion; when he appeared on the cover of *Sports Illustrated* three days later, LeBron's status as the most-publicized high school basketball player in at least a generation became established fact. Over the next year, it would become inarguable that he was the most-talked-about high school athlete ever. For now, it was enough that *SI* put him out front, his photo accompanied by the headline "The Chosen One." The issue sold out in Akron almost as soon as it hit newsstands, a collector's item in his hometown that simultaneously served as his announcement to the rest of the world. From that point on, LeBron's life was irreversibly altered; nothing he did on the court, and none of the controversy he'd eventually encounter off it, would do as much to expand his fame. As it would have been for any kid who grew up with a love of sports, making the cover of *SI* was a dream come true. It was also something of a curse.

"Y'all probably seen how crazy things have been lately with all the hype around here," he wrote in his next *SLAM* diary. "It's been crazier and crazier every day, but it don't bother me too much. I just try to block it out the best I can. The only thing that really bothered me was people selling my autograph on eBay—I was pretty mad about that . . . but it's cool. I guess that's just how people are." And it had come to this:

The kid who couldn't put down consistent back-to-back sig-natures less than a year before while eating at the Diamond Grille now saw copies of *SI*, all with his face on the cover and many with his since-refined autograph swirling across the page, selling on eBay, sometimes for triple-figure sums. Hav-ing happily signed stacks of the magazine in the weeks after it came out, LeBron was initially dismayed, then angry, to find many of them popping up on the on-line auction site. He even-tually swore off signing copies of the issue, but he found it impossible to keep the promise. He didn't like saying no to kids, and if that meant also signing for profit-minded adults on occasion, he was willing to accept it. If he didn't already know, LeBron was quickly finding out that tolerating such mi-nor annoyances had become a permanent part of his life.

If the *SI* cover confirmed his celebrity status, it also seemed to cement his place as a key marketing tool for the northeast Ohio media. The same day as the Oak Hill game, the *Cleve-land Plain Dealer* ran the first of a three-day series that de-tailed the hoopla surrounding LeBron, the money being made off his talent, and the people who were closest to him. With headlines like "The LeBron Phenomenon" and "A Peek Inside LeBron's Inner Circle," the stories in the series compared him to NBA stars as both a player and potential endorser, told of his long-shot upbringing, and explained his relationships with Gloria, Eddie, the Walkers, Coach Dru, the Fab Four, and Mav-erick Carter, his former teammate and surrogate older brother. It was the sort of detail a paper traditionally reserves for the stars of the local pro teams, offered here on a seventeen-year-old high school junior. For the rest of his prep career, LeBron would be featured almost daily in both the *Plain Dealer* and the *Akron Beacon Journal*—not to mention all the local TV and radio outlets—with the Cleveland paper eventually keeping a

"LeBron James Journal" for regular updates, and the Akron daily running a pull-out, full-color poster of LeBron at the start of his senior year. The stakes weren't as high, perhaps, but the race to see who could provide more LeBron coverage, and in turn use his name and face to sell more papers, was nearly as intense as the adidas–Nike battle for access to his feet. Soon, two or three reporters from each paper would find themselves splitting the full-time duties of the LeBron James beat.

It was all a lot to deal with, and LeBron was conscious of not letting the ever-increasing attention distract him or the Irish from achieving their goals on the court. In this case, they had a week between games—and no time to distance themselves from the *SI*-generated hype—in which to prepare for their next challenge. In yet another rematch of a game from the previous season, the Irish faced George Jr. Republic, a solid program from Pennsylvania that they'd beaten almost exactly a year earlier. The rematch would take place in Youngstown, which, as it turned out, wasn't nearly far enough from Akron to offer LeBron a breather from the spotlight. Earlier in the week, some local kids had interrupted St. V's practice in the hopes of getting LeBron's autograph on copies of the new issue of *SI*. It seemed innocent enough, until adults, some with stacks of the magazine, looking for LeBron's signature on each one, started asking for autographs, too. It was with these constant distractions—and despite the best efforts of LeBron and everyone around him, a distraction is exactly what all the attention had become—that the Irish prepared to face George Jr. Republic on the third Sunday in February.

Statistically speaking, LeBron's twenty-point, eleven-rebound effort that day wasn't bad at all. It was the outcome that left him low, a 58–57 overtime defeat that marked the first losing streak of his St. V career. There wasn't a single explanation for the loss, only a string of potential causes and missed possibilities: a horrible shooting day by the rest of the team, George Jr. Republic's depth and athleticism, and, oh yes, something about a *Sports Illustrated* cover jinx. The last of those reasons might not have carried much weight, but the intangible pressure associated with LeBron's skyrocketing fame — not to mention the all-too-tangible presence of autograph hunters and extra media at every turn — did seem to have something to do with the result. Coach Dru would admit only that LeBron seemed to have been "pressing" in the last two games; to his credit, LeBron made no excuses. "The only thing that bothers me is, I'm 16 years old and always under the microscope," he'd written in his diary a few months earlier. "I just have to watch every move I make. But I worked hard for this, I can't take it back." As he'd say again and again over the next year or so, he'd wanted this kind of success and the attention that went with it. He wasn't about to start complaining then.

Despite the loss, and the sense that the Irish, for whatever reason, appeared out of sorts on the floor, St. V claimed the state's No. 1 ranking in the final regular-season poll. The only good news about their three defeats was that all had come against out-of-state teams; through nearly three full seasons, LeBron and the rest of the Fab Four had yet to lose to an Ohio team. They maintained that streak in the final two regular-season games, convincingly dispatching Orange and Central-Hower in the final week of February. Both wins were largely unremarkable — LeBron had thirty-three points against Orange, then posted twenty-four points and twelve rebounds against Central-Hower — except for one thing. Having already drawn the ultimate compliment from the national sports media, LeBron was by then earning personal attention from some of his soon-to-be peers. The kid who had already met Antoine Walker and hung out (however briefly) with Michael Jordan was able to add another impressive name to his list when Los Angeles Lakers All-Star Shaquille O'Neal showed up to catch St. V play against Orange. The game, a 77–66 Irish victory played in nearby Canton, coincided with the Lakers' Midwest road swing; Shaq and company were scheduled to play the Cleveland Cavaliers on Thursday, but they'd arrived a day early, giving the NBA's most dominant player an off night. He chose to spend it crammed into a bleacher seat in a small Ohio gym, there to get an up-close look at the young star he'd been hearing so much about.

LeBron handled the attendance of a future Hall of Famer with typical nonchalance, saying only, "I was glad he came, but I just played my game."

Maybe so, but others reacted with a little more obvious excitement: The local papers quoted Shaq saying LeBron "deserved all the rankings he gets," while local entrepreneurs took advantage, scalping tickets for the sold-out game for three or four times their eight-dollar face value. It seemed the only person not clamoring to get into Canton Fieldhouse that night was Kobe Bryant, Shaq's Laker teammate and LeBron's likely model for an expected high-school-to-NBA jump. Though he made no effort to join Shaq in the stands at the St. V–Orange game, Kobe couldn't dodge the issue the next night, when local reporters asked him about LeBron prior to the Lakers' game against the Cavs. Queried on what advice he might give a talented young player all but certain to follow in his footsteps, Kobe's response was simple: "Do what you want."

It might not have sounded like much—and in fairness, Kobe went on to warn LeBron that college or not, he'd better be prepared to work hard whenever he got to the league— but that initial, blunt bit of guidance might have been the most inspired Kobe could have offered. As LeBron was discovering, unsolicited opinions on his game and life seemed to increase in proportion to his fame. The more well-known he become, the more he was fair game for newspaper columnists and TV and radio talking heads, most of whom had never even met him, let alone seen him play. Kobe's instruction that LeBron simply follow his heart might have seemed like throwaway advice, except that Kobe had done exactly that when he ignored the cynics six years earlier and entered the NBA draft. By any conceivable measure, that decision had turned out fairly well for Kobe; LeBron could only hope to do as well when he made up his own mind.

Heading into the 2002 state tournament, having lost more games in the past two months than they'd lost in the previous two years, the Irish had learned more about the downside of success than they'd ever wanted to know. As they'd discovered on a few occasions, most notably their near brawl with Brush High School, frustrated opponents would sometimes resort to cheap shots to counter St. V's talent. More and more, they were also finding out that as much as they were a popular draw at the ticket office, selling out nearly every gym they played, a surprising number of those "fans" were anything but fans of the Irish. Coach Dru had said as much after his team's victory over Orange, commending his team's resolve despite the fact that "many of the fans were here to see us lose." LeBron, as he made clear in his next *SLAM* diary, saw it too.

"It's strange, 'cause almost every game feels like a road game for us," he wrote. "I'd say three-fourths of the people are rooting for us to lose most games. Everybody wants to see the giants fall, I guess, but I love it when people are against me. I want that."

Certainly, the whole state of Ohio seemed to be gunning for St. V as the Irish opened the defense of their consecutive state titles. The goal was simple: Go 7–0 in the month of March, as they'd done in each of the past two years, and the trophy, the rings, and the bragging rights would once again be theirs. Their first one came easily enough, a 107–47 blowout of Firelands in the opening round. Next came a rematch with Archbishop Hoban, the local Catholic rival they'd beat a month earlier. Perhaps spurred by the rivalry, or maybe just looking for some kind of mental edge against a superior team, the Hoban players came out for pregame warm-ups wearing T-shirts with "The Chosen One," a mockery of the *Sports Illustrated* cover line, printed on the front in big letters. It might have been enough to rattle a lesser player, but for LeBron, it only served as motivation. Despite Hoban's physical defense, he scored an easy twenty points as St. V rolled to a 72–33 win.

Three days later, the Irish faced another familiar foe, this time the Central-Hower team they'd knocked off just two weeks earlier, in their regular-season finale. The first meeting between the teams had been fairly competitive; this one was even closer. St. V actually trailed by a point in the final minutes, but a strong finish and LeBron's thirty-two points proved sufficient, and the Irish eked out a 66–61 victory. That win set up a regional semifinal matchup with Warrensville

Heights, to be played at Cleveland's Gund Arena. Home of the NBA's Cavaliers, whose recent losing ways meant they usually drew well under capacity, the Gund would draw an unusually full house for this battle. By the time the stubs had been counted, 20,562 fans—a sellout and by far a record for a high school basketball game in Ohio—were packed into the gym to see St. V pummel Warrensville Heights, 78–49. LeBron was solid, if comparatively quiet, tallying a near triple-double of sixteen points, eleven rebounds, and eight assists. Meanwhile, his classmate and good friend, Romeo Travis, scored a career-high thirty-one points to lead the rout. Two weeks into the state tournament, it was four down, three to go, and the Irish appeared to be regaining their championship form.

Nothing changed in the regional title game three days later, a 77–58 win over Ottawa-Glandorf, or in the state semifinals, a 76–36 blowout of Poland Seminary that came five days after that. Despite everything—the two-game losing streak, the defensive lapses, the pressure and the off-court distractions— St. V was on an indisputable roll, having won eight straight going into the state title game. Confidence was high, especially with Romeo and the rest of the Irish playing terrific in LeBron's shadow; given those back-to-back titles, experience was on St. V's side, too. All the Irish had to do was win one more game.

Turns out, they picked the wrong team for that task.

Their state-final opponent, as many figured it might be, was Roger Bacon, the parochial power from Cincinnati that had played St. V close before dropping a nine-point decision in December. This time, in front of a sellout crowd of 18,375 at Ohio State's Value City Arena, Roger Bacon worked harder on the boards, took better care of the ball, and shared the offensive load more efficiently than their Irish counterparts. The result, despite thirty-two points from LeBron, was a 71–63 victory for Roger Bacon. For LeBron and the Fab Four, it was their first loss to an Ohio team; far more painfully, it was their first season without a state championship. The Irish finished the season 23–4, and LeBron won his second straight Mr. Basketball award—and right about then, all of that had to feel pretty empty. As he admitted after the fact, LeBron had been far from a hundred percent healthy in the state final; but he wouldn't use it as an excuse, and in truth, it probably wouldn't have mattered. As had been the case a few other times that season, St. V simply hadn't been the best team on the floor.

Looking back more than a year later, LeBron admitted that his difficult junior season—and that state final loss in particular—accounted for the greatest disappointment in his young basketball career. But, as was typical for a young man who seemed to take every setback as a personal challenge, he credited that relative failure with spurring him to greater success. "I think it made us a better team," he said in hindsight, "because we knew how it felt, and we knew we didn't want it to happen again. We were not the team that we could've been. We were distracted by a lot of things . . . I just think we weren't really focused, and I don't know the reason why, but we can really see it when we look back on the team."

To his credit, LeBron never once looked for excuses to explain away St. V's unsatisfying '01–02 season. He could have pointed to the unrealistic expectations placed on him and the team, especially with a first-year head coach at the helm. He could have blamed the unyielding media scrutiny, or the often-chaotic scenes created whenever fans, autograph seekers, and the merely curious converged in his name. He might have reminded cynics of what he'd written in his diary just a month or so before, how he was "16 years old and always under the microscope." But he did none of that, choosing instead to take much of the blame himself. "That was on me as a leader," he acknowledged months later. Even if it wasn't solely on him—and even if the Irish might never have gotten close to a high school three-peat without him—LeBron's admission was telling. Anyone who'd been paying attention to his progress could see that LeBron had worked hard for his success, and that, increasingly, he was capable of handling the intense pressure that went with it. The more elusive traits for a seventeen-year-old celebrity athlete were the wisdom and sense of responsibility needed to carry the blame when his ample supplies of talent and confidence somehow weren't enough to keep things from going wrong. Combined, all these qualities added up to a very specific sum. They made LeBron James a leader, in the truest sense of the word.

It was there, most obviously, in how he played his best in the biggest games, leading by example on the court. It was there in the way he credited his teammates in every interview—a cliché, perhaps, but one those teammates no doubt appreciated. Call it leading with a nudge; it made them feel respected, reminded them of their worth. It was there in more subtle ways, too, even off the court. After he'd completed his high school career, one shoe company rep recalled, LeBron was at dinner with a large group that included family members, a few teammates and friends, and a mixed crew of the free-spending sneaker company execs and player agents who were still courting LeBron. As the rep remembered, "As usual, LeBron just took over, asking us, 'Who are you paying for?' Around the room like that, 'Okay, who are *you* paying for?'

Then telling his friends, 'Okay, you guys are covered by them, and you guys are covered by him, and you guys . . . I don't know who got you.' "

Maybe most important, it came naturally to him; after all, this was a kid who had joined a talented, senior-laden St. V team as a freshman and essentially claimed it as his own. "I don't know, it's just . . . the love for what I do," he'd explain a year later, near the end of his high school career, "I just always want to be a leader. If I'm playing football, I'm the leader of my team and I want to win. If I'm playing basketball, I'm the leader and I want to win. I just think that I want to be the leader at whatever I do, and I feel that the people I'm around, when I say let's do this or do that, they know I'm not telling 'em nothin' wrong."

Just two days after the unhappy completion of his junior season, LeBron was showing off another admirable trait: his sense of the bigger picture.

Understandably exhausted by the stress of the season and all the distractions it brought, he nonetheless kept a promise to attend an autograph signing at a local mall. The event, organized by Chris Dennis, drew hundreds of fans, some of whom waited in line nearly ten hours to get LeBron's signature. Though he arrived late for the scheduled autograph session, LeBron signed for two hours, as promised, inking photos, T-shirts, and basketballs—pretty much anything but copies of his *Sports Illustrated* cover story—for fans who'd paid for the chance to meet the young star. Proceeds went to a local youth charity; even as his growing celebrity status increasingly took the fun out of such public appearances in the coming year, LeBron continued to participate whenever kids' charities were involved.

Besides showing his rarely reported selflessness, his attendance at the charity autograph signing was significant in one other way: It was LeBron's last scheduled turn in the public eye until the summer hoop season, which would begin in earnest a few months later. Ideally, he could have used those last weeks of his junior year of high school to unwind away from reporters and fans and profiteers, to concentrate on school and hanging out with his friends. By then, though, LeBron should have known better than to think he would be able to stay out of the spotlight for long.

Chapter Eight

As months go, April 2002 started out fairly well for LeBron James. With his second straight Ohio Mr. Basketball award already secure, he found himself clearing even more room on his trophy shelf, adding the prestigious Parade and Gatorade national player of the year awards to his impressive haul. Both were notable honors—he was the first junior ever to claim the Gatorade award—but they'd be the last bit of purely good news he'd hear for a while.

In mid-April, right around the time LeBron was accepting the Gatorade award, rumors began to circulate that he was planning to spend his senior season somewhere other than St. Vincent–St. Mary High School. Some pointed to his friendship with Carmelo Anthony as a sign that LeBron would transfer to Oak Hill Academy, the well-known basketball factory that had churned out dozens of top college and NBA players. The fact that Carmelo was graduating and therefore wouldn't be around to play with his good friend seemed an obvious wrench in any such theory, but that didn't slow the gossip. The more fantastic story had LeBron, Glo, and Eddie packing up and moving overseas—Italy was most often mentioned as a likely destination—to spend his senior season playing professional basketball in Europe.

LeBron dunks during a photo shoot for *SLAM* magazine, May 2001. PHOTOGRAPH COURTESY OF ATIBA JEFFERSON

LeBron photographed behind the St. Vincent–St. Mary campus for *SLAM* magazine, May 2001. PHOTOGRAPH COURTESY OF ATIBA JEFFERSON

LeBron attacks the rim during the 2001 adidas ABCD Camp. PHOTOGRAPH COURTESY OF ADIDAS

LeBron meets the press at the 2002 adidas ABCD Camp. Though he sat out the camp with a broken left wrist, his attendance was a huge draw for fans and media alike. PHOTOGRAPH COURTESY OF ADIDAS

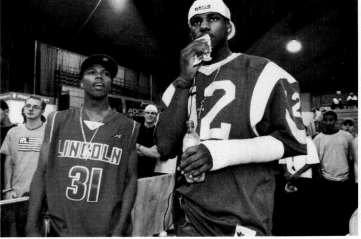

LeBron (right) with good friend and fellow high school All-American Sebastian Telfair at the 2002 adidas ABCD Camp. Though a broken wrist kept him from participating, LeBron was the camp's biggest draw. PHOTOGRAPH COURTESY OF JENNIFER POTTHEISER

LeBron photographed for *SLAM* magazine, May 2002. PHOTOGRAPH COURTESY OF CLAY PATRICK MCBRIDE

LeBron photographed for *SLAM* magazine, May 2002. PHOTOGRAPH COURTESY OF CLAY PATRICK MCBRIDE

LeBron photographed for *SLAM* magazine, May 2002. PHOTOGRAPH COURTESY OF CLAY PATRICK MCBRIDE

A sweatshirt and T-shirt with early adidas logos for LeBron. The "King James 3XL Ballah" tag with a crown and his number 23 is visible at the bottom of each. PHOTOGRAPH COURTESY OF RUSS BENGTSON

One of the custom-made wristbands LeBron wore throughout his senior year at St. Vincent–St. Mary. This one references the cover line from his appearance on the cover of *Sports Illustrated*. PHOTOGRAPH COURTESY OF RUSS BENGTSON

Cardboard cutouts like these, handed out at games during LeBron's senior year, often ended up on eBay along with hundreds of other LeBron-related items available for online auction on any given day. PHOTOGRAPH COURTESY OF RUSS BENGTSON

One of LeBron's St. Vincent–St. Mary jerseys, worn during his senior year. The designers at adidas took LeBron's input on much of their gear over his final two seasons. PHOTOGRAPH COURTESY OF RUSS BENGTSON

An adidas Pro Model shoe, customized for LeBron to wear during his senior year at St. Vincent–St.Mary. PHOTOGRAPH COURTESY OF SALLY BERMAN

LeBron interviewed by ESPN's Jay Bilas after St. Vincent–St. Mary's nationally televised victory over Mater Dei in January 2003. Photograph courtesy of Atiba Jefferson

LeBron restrains teammate Romeo Travis during St. Vincent's game against Mater Dei in January 2003. More than a superior talent, LeBron was a natural leader from virtually the first game of his high school career. Photograph courtesy of Atiba Jefferson

LeBron wipes the sweat from his face during St. Vincent's game against Mater Dei in January 2003. Top executives from Nike and adidas showed up in force for the game, a fact LeBron silently acknowledges with the competing logos on his shorts. Photograph courtesy of Atiba Jefferson

Two of the billboards adidas leased in Akron in May of 2003 in a last-ditch effort to convince LeBron to sign with the three stripes. Though adidas put the most personal attention into their efforts to sign LeBron, the money offered by Nike proved too much to ignore. PHOTOGRAPH COURTESY OF ADIDAS

LeBron, head-to-toe in adidas gear, poses in front of the Michael Jordan statue outside of Chicago's United Center. The NBA legend and Nike endorser was one of Nike's biggest weapons in its pursuit of LeBron. PHOTOGRAPH COURTESY OF ADIDAS

LeBron poses with Sonny Vaccaro of adidas before the 2003 Roundball Classic in Chicago. Vaccaro is the man credited with revolutionizing the sneaker industry and the business of basketball over the last 25 years. PHOTOGRAPH COURTESY OF ADIDAS

LeBron skies for a dunk en route to winning MVP of the 2003 Roundball Classic in Chicago. He also won MVP awards at the McDonald's and Capital Classic postseason all-star games. PHOTOGRAPH COURTESY OF ADIDAS

LeBron takes a breather during the 2003 Roundball Classic in Chicago. PHOTOGRAPH COURTESY OF ADIDAS

LeBron throws down a dunk en route to winning the MVP award in the 2003 McDonald's All-American Game at Cleveland's Gund Arena. Six months later, "The Gund" would be his home gym during his rookie NBA season with the Cavs. PHOTOGRAPH COURTESY OF STAN HONDA/McDONALD'S ALL-AMERICAN GAME

With both rumors, some shortsighted "logic" was presented: by transferring to Oak Hill or some such similar school
with a grueling schedule and national name recognition,
LeBron could regularly play with and against better competition and increase his own visibility in the process; or, by going
to Europe, he could circumvent the NBA's rule barring high
school underclassmen from entering its draft and cash in on
his game and fame right away, making his NBA debut a year
later. The fact that the same shoe companies currently pur-
suing him also sponsored some of the top European club
teams—and could therefore sweeten the deal if LeBron
actually ended up overseas—made it sound almost feasible.

The problems with both theories were numerous. Oak Hill
was unquestionably a terrific program with an enviable tradition of preparing its basketball alumni for future success;
had LeBron transferred, he would have indeed faced great
competition, and the team would have drawn plenty of attention. But then, weren't both things already true at St. V? Since
LeBron's arrival, the Irish themselves had played one of the
tougher schedules in the nation—so tough, they'd played Oak
Hill twice, and were scheduled to face them again early in
LeBron's senior year. As for increased recognition, it was hard
to imagine that was even possible where LeBron was concerned. He was, after all, the kid whose face had appeared
on the cover of *Sports Illustrated* just a few months before,
and whose name was already penciled in as the No. 1 pick in
the 2003 NBA draft by almost anyone with an opinion. And
even if he could have gotten more exposure, did he really
need it?

In some ways, the Europe rumor seemed less absurd, if
only because of the money that would allegedly be involved.
Some whispers claimed that between a deal with, say, a top

Italian club team, combined with the money adidas or Nike could throw in to secure his endorsement rights, a single season of pro basketball in Italy might be worth $20 million or more to LeBron before he ever stepped onto an NBA court. It seemed almost conceivable, which is ironic, considering that there's no reason to believe any such offer was ever made. Though LeBron wasn't initially asked about the rumors, they were flatly denied both by Coach Dru and Eddie Jackson. "I just talked to LeBron," Coach Dru told *USA Today,* "and he was working out and talking about winning another state championship." Eddie was even more blunt. "Not only have we not heard a $9 million offer, we haven't heard a $100 offer," he told *SLAM.* "We haven't even heard anybody say they're interested. Actually, I don't even know the names of the teams over there."

Unfortunately for LeBron, his family and St. V, no number of denials were enough of a deterrent for those looking to use his name to create a buzz for themselves. The Italy rumor apparently originated from an upstart basketball website whose "story" lacked any sort of attribution or sources to back it up; the fact that it was subsequently picked up by national media outlets that probably should have known better shows how big a story LeBron had become. What both rumors—and others that would sprout up over the coming year—had in common was a lack of any factual foundation and an ability to spread like wildfire. They couldn't have existed if LeBron's tale wasn't so compelling, and by their existence, they made that saga that much more fascinating to the millions of people who were already watching. For LeBron himself, it was all just one more distraction he'd learn to get used to, part of the price to be paid for success.

As it was, there were still plenty of perks to being LeBron, one of which, in late April, was a weekend trip to New York City. A year after his first national feature appeared in *SLAM*, LeBron would be featured on the magazine's cover alongside his good friend Sebastian Telfair. As arguably the best senior- and junior-to-be in the nation—and undoubtedly the two most publicized prep players in America, regardless of class— they'd be the first-ever high schoolers to grace a *SLAM* cover. The shared cover made sense not only for those reasons, but because LeBron and Sebastian had become close friends since first meeting the previous summer, keeping in touch with regular phone calls and two-way pages. As LeBron had written in one of his *SLAM* diaries earlier in the season, "ABCD Camp was the first time I saw him. He impressed me a lot, and I got much respect for him. He's a great player and a good friend."

The photo shoot and interview were scheduled for Saturday afternoon, but LeBron, Gloria, Eddie, and Maverick flew in Friday evening, just in time for LeBron to make an appearance at IS8, a middle school in Queens whose cramped, yellow-lit gym was home to some of the best off-season prep basketball in all of New York. The runs at IS8 were local legend, a secret shared by Big Apple basketball cognoscenti who came to see the city's best high school players, aligned with various AAU and club teams, in heated competition in the spring and early summer. Historically, nearly all of New York's best young players had proven themselves there, and even out-of-town stars had occasionally tested themselves in the IS8 crucible. But few, if any, of those previous visitors carried LeBron's name recognition, so it wasn't surprising that rumors (justified, this time) of his attendance spread quickly among the hard-core NYC hoop community. Invited by Sebastian to play with his Juice All-Stars team that weekend, LeBron agreed, arriving at the gym directly from the airport, changing into a uniform, and stepping into the starting lineup. Despite the numerous out-of-state appearances he'd make in his high school career, both with St. V and at various camps and all-star games, this two-night stand at IS8 would mark the only time LeBron would play in New York City—until he joined the NBA.

In truth, his initial experience wasn't all that memorable. He'd spent most of the day crammed into cars and airplanes and had virtually no time to loosen up before taking the court, hardly the ideal circumstances for any basketball player, especially one hoping to prove himself in front of a hard-to-impress crowd of basketball aficionados. In the course of an easy win—one paced largely by Sebastian's highlight-filled night—LeBron wasn't bad at all; he just wasn't his usual unstoppable self. His good-but-not-great performance generated mixed reviews among those in attendance, something LeBron admitted he was aware of. "You know, my shot wasn't falling, so I passed the ball," he said the next day. "I mean, I'll keep shooting, 'cause most shooters kept shooting, but if I'm not on my game, I still find way to help my team win—which we did."

In the wake of that subpar showing, many assumed LeBron had simply been affected by the pressure of his surroundings. Given the noisy, standing-room-only crowd that lined the gym, often just a few inches off the sidelines, it was a rare player who wouldn't have been distracted or intimidated—but as he'd proven in front of so many other expectant crowds, LeBron was among the rarest. The more likely explanation echoed something his old high school coach, Keith Dambrot, had said about LeBron a year earlier. "One of the things that's unique about this guy," Dambrot had said, "is that he's better in structure than he is in pickup." In other words, many great players, especially at the high school level, often struggle to play well within a team concept because they're surrounded with inferior teammates. The temptation to rely on their individual talent at the expense of involving their teammates can be hard to ignore, and the emphasis on one-on-one offensive play—something that's driven into the minds of young players through countless ESPN highlights, video games, and the growing popularity of "streetball" style—makes it that much harder. All of which explains why LeBron, teamed with players he'd never played with in a game full of one-on-one battles, didn't dominate his initial IS8 run—although he returned the next night, loose and more familiar with his teammates, and played much better in a narrow loss to the Long Island Panthers AAU squad. It also explains why NBA scouts, who know that the best players in their league are those who can bring their teammates up to their level, raved so loudly about LeBron's game.

His first impression of New York City basketball was only one of the topics covered the following day, when LeBron met up with Sebastian in the gym of a small college in midtown Manhattan for an interview and photo shoot. Of greater interest was LeBron's take on the rumors that had him spending his senior year of high school overseas, something he'd hadn't yet discussed in the media. Confirming what everyone around him had already said, "I didn't see it at first," he said. "People kept two-waying me and asking me, 'Did I see something about Italy.' And I was like, Nah . . . You know, it came out of nowhere, and there's nobody who talked to us and our family. So that was just a false statement."

What he didn't do was refute the possibility that, if a multimillion-dollar offer had been made, he and his family would have considered it. "I don't think it's an option, 'cause

I've got a lot of friends and family back home," LeBron said. He paused for a second, then continued with a laugh. "But, hey, if they offer something. I mean, it's kind of hard to make a decision when it's not really in front of you. But I think I'll probably stay in high school and stay with the school I've been with for three years."

Asked the same question later in the day, Gloria echoed her son's admission that they'd be crazy not to at least think about such an offer if it had ever been made. Both mother and son knew all too well what it was like to live day to day, without anything resembling financial security, and LeBron's earning potential was an almost blinding light at the end of their tunnel. They still lived in the same low-income housing development—a small, top-floor, corner apartment in Akron's Spring Hill complex—and were far from wealthy. With help from Eddie and other family and friends, LeBron and Gloria were getting along comfortably, but it would have been hard to blame them for wanting to listen to any offer that might have left them set for life before LeBron had even finished school. But, as everyone involved had by then made clear, LeBron was staying put, and there were more relevant issues to discuss—like how he was handling the increased media attention and everything that came with it. A year earlier, when LeBron had done his first interview with *SLAM*, he was pulled out of class to meet the interviewer, and someone had placed a small sign in front of the school building that read WELCOME SLAM MAGAZINE. Not long after, the school would hire a full-time public relations liaison and bar the media from campus during school hours. His success, and the media's coverage of it, had been just that dramatic, and there had been no more drastic a change in his life over the past year. Asked about it, LeBron acknowledged the relentlessness of all that attention, but, as always, he refused to complain. "Of course it's been real crazy," he said. "At home, you can't barely walk out the door without somebody asking you for an autograph and wanting to talk to you, give you advice. As of right now, it's all right. Everybody's chillin' because the season's over. But, you know, I like it, and I'm gonna just keep working hard and keep trying to make it to where I'm trying to get."

He had mixed feelings on how persistent that attention would be in the coming year. "I think it's gonna get crazy, but you never know," he said. "It might calm down, especially when I make the decision between going to college and going to the NBA . . . or it might get crazier then."

A year had passed since the initial eruption of interest in his future plans, and the longer he waited to make his decision public, the more attention there figured to be. Perhaps already aware of that fact, LeBron hinted strongly at how that decision would turn out. A year before he would make it official, LeBron acknowledged it was unlikely he'd ever play college basketball. "Realistically, probably not, because of how things are moving right now," he said. "But it can change. Things can happen, things that could have to *make* me go to college. And you can't control things like that. Things can happen, and the things that might happen, I can't change."

Knowing the off-court issues would be taken care of as along as he remained at his best on the court, LeBron spoke at length about his improvement over the past year, and about the progress still to be made in his game. "I think I've got a more complete game," he said. "I'm hitting my outside jumpers consistently, making my teammates better, and my strength has improved, and my post game has improved. For the future, I'm improving on my outside shot right now, and my ball-handling skills are getting better. I'm not the flashy-type ball handler, but I can get the job done. I just want to keep working on things, my upper-body strength, my lower-body strength, and just make sure I'll be ready for the next level."

There was another side of that weekend in New York that had nothing to do with photo shoots and interviews. Since both LeBron and Sebastian played for adidas-sponsored high school teams, the shoe company had helped arrange the trip from Ohio. Partly, it was a matter of convenience, but it also gave representatives from adidas a chance to spend the weekend with LeBron, further cementing their relationship while, at least for a few days, keeping hard-charging Nike at bay. At least two potential agents were in town as well, subtly making their presence felt when LeBron, Sebastian, and a dozen or so family, friends, and adidas reps went out Friday night after the IS8 game for a late dinner at Justin's, the midtown Manhattan restaurant owned by Sean "Puffy" Combs.

Over the previous year, there had been a few similar gatherings in the pursuit of LeBron's business alliances; over the coming year, there would be many, many more, both in Akron and around the country. But this one—the entire weekend, in fact—was notable because, like that weekend in Oakland a year earlier, it served as a "barometer" of sorts, measuring (and even helping determine) the scale of the LeBron James courtship. As one of the agents who sat in on that Friday night dinner said, "That weekend, for the *SLAM* cover shoot, it didn't change much publicly, but in the scope of the sneaker battle it had a huge impact. Just the way people were taken care of on that trip, including the entourages, with dinners, gear, hotels . . . it took everything to the next level."

For the average observer, the only sign of adidas's ratcheted-up efforts that weekend were personalized patent-leather green Pro Models LeBron wore for the photo shoot, with the gold embroidered "LJ23" visible in a full-page photo that ran in the *SLAM* feature. But it was the behind-the-scenes efforts that had a real impact; if, in the words of that anonymous shoe industry insider, they had "created the monster" a year earlier, this weekend represented the creature's growth spurt. The result, as that agent saw it, was that "You can't impress this kid anymore. You've always gotta keep coming up with something *more*." That was the situation that adidas and Nike, as well as potential agents and any other prospective business partners, now found themselves in. Even where the stakes were lower, the pressure to make an impression was intense, a fact that only become more undeniable over the next twelve months.

"The limo company that they used that weekend, we still use them when we're in New York," the anonymous agent said a year later, shortly before the 2003 draft. "I spoke to the driver recently, and I told him he's gotta make sure he gets LeBron's business for the draft. And the driver says, 'I know, I know, I gotta come up with something new . . . I think I'm gonna have to come out with the helicopter.' He was only half-joking."

The potential payout after all this one-upmanship was no laughing matter—the most prominent whispers were that LeBron's shoe deal, still a year away from being signed, would be worth *at least* $10 million a year, and quite possibly more. Whatever LeBron himself might be worth, there were other factors affecting the numbers that would eventually end up on his contract. Just days after the *SLAM* photo shoot, adidas announced that it had signed Tracy McGrady to a "lifetime" deal; the Orlando Magic star was already under contract with the company, and the new deal would ensure he would stay with adidas at least until his playing career ended. That announcement came less than a year after Reebok indefinitely extended the contract of its top endorser, Allen Iverson—and, at almost the same time, rumors surfaced that adidas endorser Kobe Bryant was unhappy with his contract and would soon opt out, most likely to sign a deal with Nike. All of this seemed to work to the benefit of LeBron, whose endorsement potential was seen as on par with all of the above, and maybe even equal to Michael Jordan's. *Potential* was, of course, the operative word, but given his dynamic playing style, the sort of hard-knock upbringing that gave Iverson so much "street" appeal, and the fact that, with Jordan finally retired for good, the shoe industry seemed eager for an iconic figure to replace him, LeBron was very much the right man at the right time.

A few months earlier, shortly before LeBron's *Sports Illustrated* cover hit the street, the head of a noted sports marketing firm was quoted as saying that LeBron would get only a fraction of what Kobe Bryant and Tracy McGrady had received from adidas when they first arrived in the NBA. "A faceless high school player can't do anything for the shoe companies . . . Athletes are not reaping endorsement money right out of the box. That's not good for high school players. They really have to earn their stripes."

He couldn't have known how wrong he was.

LeBron finished out his junior year in relative peace, traveling occasionally for AAU games with both Oakland Slam-N-Jam and the Michigan Hurricanes, another adidas-affiliated AAU program; by all accounts, he was as impressive as ever, especially in a run with Slam-N-Jam in Houston. Playing alongside fellow prep All-American candidates Kendrick Perkins of Texas and Leon Powe of California, LeBron was even more remarkable than usual. Chris Rivers, the adidas rep who followed LeBron throughout his high school career, put it bluntly: "He was amazing. I still say that's the best he's ever played." He added yet another award to his collection, as he was named the *USA Today* national player of the year. By the third week of May, it appeared he might go an entire month without any sort of controversy. But, once again, staying out of the news proved impossible for LeBron.

John Lucas, the head coach of the Cleveland Cavaliers and by then a friend of LeBron and his family, came to St. V's season-ending banquet in late June as a guest speaker. Though he'd already been reprimanded by the NBA—which liked talking about high school players almost as much as it liked drafting them—nearly a year earlier for discussing LeBron at another speech, Lucas nonetheless joked with the Irish's team MVP during his address. It was no secret that the Cavs, and Lucas in particular, were in love with the idea of drafting LeBron; it would give the struggling franchise a difference-maker on the court and a huge marketing draw for a team that regularly played in front of half-empty home crowds. Lucas made no attempt to keep those feelings secret, but this time, apparently, no one in the NBA office seemed to mind.

David Stern and Co. did take exception a few days later, however, when Lucas invited LeBron to a voluntary workout organized by the Cavaliers. Among the participants were about half the Cavs' roster, as well as a number of local college players and some free agents hoping to catch on with NBA teams. Had it gone off quietly, it likely wouldn't have caused a problem; instead, it was prominently reported in the local media, including a story in the *Cleveland Plain Dealer* that quoted Lucas saying, "We got to have him," after LeBron shook a defender and threw down a spectacular reverse dunk. Afterward, his NBA veteran opponents were unanimous in their praise of LeBron's talent and maturity, and one former NBA assistant who attended the workout raved, "Instead of looking out of place being out there with NBA players, he looked like one of them. He fit right in." And the problem? Only that LeBron's participation in the workout violated NBA rules "prohibiting contact between NBA teams and players not yet eligible for the draft," as the league's bylaws worded it. The result—as one AP writer wittily put it, "LeBron James has drawn his first NBA foul, and it cost the Cleveland Cavaliers"—was that the Cavs were fined $150,000, and Lucas was suspended from coaching the first two games of the 2002–03 season. For Lucas and the Cavs, the situation was rather ridiculous—especially since it was common knowledge that Lucas had done the same with Kobe Bryant when he was the coach of the Philadelphia Sixers and Kobe was a Philadelphia-area high school senior in the mid-nineties.

There was also an apparent double standard in place, since LeBron had played in Michael Jordan's highly publicized pickup games the previous summer; at the time, Jordan hadn't yet made his comeback announcement official, but he was a member of the Washington Wizards' front office. Regardless, while the situation was another headache for a Cavs organization that had had more than its share, it only added to LeBron's ever-growing reputation. The Cavs were the ones who had broken a rule—all LeBron had done was hold his own, and then some, against a bunch of NBA vets.

Given his proven ability to perform well against actual NBA

players, LeBron figured to be more dominant than ever against his pending summer schedule of AAU and all-star camp competition. The highlights of his summer calendar included potential runs with Slam-N-Jam, the Hurricanes, and the local Shooting Stars, as well as return trips to the adidas-sponsored Big Time Tournament and ABCD Camp. "I'm just trying to prove I'm the best player in the country," he wrote in one of his final *SLAM* diaries. "But I don't want to do too much. The people who've seen me know that I can play the game. I've established myself, and as of this point, all I can do is fall."

He was right, of course. Doing too much—playing a full May-to-August schedule as so many high school players did in an effort to prove themselves—made no sense for LeBron James in the summer of 2002. He was already the consensus best high school basketball player in America, all but a shoo-in to be the No. 1 pick in the 2003 NBA draft. He needed to keep working, of course, to keep getting stronger and fine-tune his game, but he didn't need a nonstop national summer tour for that. Indeed, it probably wouldn't have been a bad idea to take most of the summer off—which, in a way, is exactly what he did. And when it was over, he was somehow bigger than ever.

Chapter Nine

By the time LeBron James graduated from high school, the city of Chicago had been home to some of the most memorable moments of his life. It's where he first met his basketball idol, Michael Jordan, and his favorite rapper, Jay-Z. At the end of his senior year, it would be one of three stops he'd make on the postseason all-star circuit. And in June of 2002, in what would become arguably the most difficult month of his young life, it would be the place where all his hopes and dreams were nearly dashed for good.

On Saturday, June 8, LeBron was playing with the Northeast Ohio Shooting Stars at an AAU tournament at Chicago's Julian High School. A number of NBA scouts and players, including the Suns' Shawn Marion, the Bulls' Eddy Curry, and soon-to-be Cavalier Darius Miles, were there to take in the game. The Shooting Stars held a big lead midway through the second half when LeBron went strong to the basket, clearly intending to dunk. The only thing between him and an easy two was CJ Walleck, a forward for the Chicago Rising Stars. Caught in an awkward position, somewhere between trying to take a charge and get out of the way, Walleck unintentionally undercut LeBron, who had already left his feet. LeBron landed hard, absorbing much of the impact on his left wrist. Clearly in pain, he stayed on the floor. By the time an ambulance had delivered him to a nearby hospital, it was confirmed: His wrist was broken, and his summer, at least on the basketball court, was essentially over.

It was a scary incident all the way around. Walleck, who by all accounts had simply reacted poorly and meant no harm, was first ejected from the game, then harassed and even threatened by some fans before leaving the gym. For LeBron, of course, the fear had more to do with the long term. A serious enough break could have jeopardized his career, meaning all the hard work he'd put in, and all the drama he'd already endured, might have been for naught. The good news came fairly quickly, though: Doctors told LeBron that while he wouldn't be able to play for six to eight weeks, the injury wouldn't require surgery and wasn't expected to have any long-term effects.

His treatment would eventually be handled by a former Chicago Bulls team physician, and eleven days after the injury, he would return to Chicago to have a hard cast placed on his nonshooting wrist. All in all, it could have been much worse, and it was generally agreed that the injury would do nothing to affect his status as the likely top pick in the 2003 draft. His next break—a figurative one in this case—wouldn't heal so quickly.

Less than two weeks after LeBron broke his wrist, the *Cleveland Plain Dealer* reported that Eddie Jackson, the father figure whom LeBron seemed to grow closer to all the time, and who had taken an increasingly involved role in LeBron's life, was to be indicted on fraud charges. Though the alleged crimes had nothing to do with LeBron, the indictment was front-page news in Akron only because Eddie, who'd served time for a drug conviction in the early nineties, was so publicly identified with the nation's top prep basketball player. As bad as it was for Eddie, who was facing time in federal prison if convicted, the charges were yet another curveball for LeBron, who would pledge his support to Eddie at every turn. Over the next year, the word "adversity" would become one of his favorites whenever someone asked about his life: how much of it he'd seen growing up and how he welcomed the challenge. That attitude would rarely serve him better than it was about to.

With so many distractions—his left arm in a cast nearly up to his elbow, his "dad" facing a trial and probable prison time—as a backdrop, LeBron went about his amended summer schedule. With his broken wrist keeping him out of uniform, a relatively quiet "off-season" seemed possible, maybe even likely. Instead, without ever playing a game, LeBron made more noise in the space of a few days than most players make in a lifetime. Unsurprisingly, the adidas–Nike battle had more than a little to do with that.

A number of factors led to the circus that occurred in the first two weeks of July, and LeBron was at its center. His injury had left him unable to play at ABCD Camp, but that didn't mean adidas didn't want him to show up anyway; his attendance at camp would be a huge boost for publicity, for which there was a void with LeBron out of action. Of course, the folks at Nike had high hopes of LeBron attending their annual All-American Camp as well. Had he been healthy and able to play, LeBron would have had to choose one over the other, as the camps essentially ran concurrently. In fact, Nike started a few days earlier, and ABCD ended a few days later, but they overlapped in the middle, meaning it was essentially impossible to compete in both. And while it was hardly unheard of for players to switch allegiances and, at the last second, back out of one camp to attend the other—and while Nike certainly did everything it could to influence LeBron to do just that— he was, by all accounts, committed to attend the adidas camp. But all that assumed he was playing, and of course, he wasn't—so why couldn't he attend both? It was a question made that much more intriguing when Maverick Carter came into play.

Until this point, Maverick had played a largely below-the-radar role in LeBron's life. Though not actually related, they called each other "cousin" and were as close as brothers. Having moved back to Akron after a year at Western Michigan, the young man known to friends and family as "Mav" was attending Akron U. and planned to play for the Zips basketball team the following season. The chance to return home, and to play for his former St. V coach and current Akron assistant, Keith Dambrot, were big draws for Mav, but by the summer of 2002, his role as LeBron's right-hand man was becoming an almost full-time job. That job was vaguely defined and all-encompassing, all at once: he was part security guard, part PR man, part workout partner, and part confidant. Just three years LeBron's senior, he was old enough—and possessed a sharp enough basketball mind—to have earned LeBron's respect both on and off the court. He'd help out at St. V practices and work LeBron individually, sharing his knowledge and demanding effort and intensity from the young man he was already calling "The Golden Child."

"He's probably the best leader that I've ever played with," LeBron had said a year earlier when asked about Mav, who'd been St. V's star senior when LeBron was a freshman. "He's not a big-time scorer, but just the kind of player that gets it done."

By the summer of 2002, Mav was something else: an intern

at Nike. The fact had been reported in *Sports Illustrated,* among other places, notable because it was seen by many as one of the more cunning moves yet in the chess game to sign LeBron. Whatever impact Mav's work with Nike may have had on LeBron's loyalties is a matter of speculation, but the fact was that, with both companies in hot pursuit and his potential worth seemingly going up by the second, it was in LeBron's best interests financially to encourage the competition. And by showing up at both the Nike and adidas camps in July of 2002, LeBron did exactly that.

His trip to Indianapolis for the Nike camp was relatively quiet, especially when compared with the ruckus he'd stir up at ABCD a few days later. Because of Nike's more stringent PR policies, the press was kept largely away from LeBron and his family when he made an appearance—reportedly wearing adidas sneakers—at the Nike-run event. A day later, he popped up in the far-less-constrained environment at adidas, and almost immediately, the circus was in full effect. The moment he walked into the Fairleigh Dickinson University gym late on the second-to-last day of camp, things were different; there was no denying that a celebrity had arrived. He came in through a side door with Eddie and a few friends, and while four full-court games continued on the wide hardwood floor, the room's attention immediately and almost universally shifted to the corner of the gym. Some of the camp participants, who knew LeBron through various encounters on the camp and AAU circuit, approached to say what's up. Spectators ignored the games and focused on LeBron—sharp in a custom jersey, fitted hat, and pristine white Nikes—as he made his way along the sidelines to a spot in the bleachers. Even the campers who were actually playing games at the time weren't immune; during timeouts, more than a few could be seen looking LeBron's way.

Two of LeBron's St. V teammates, Romeo Travis and Dru Joyce III, were invited to ABCD Camp that year and were playing when LeBron arrived. Settling into a wooden bleacher seat, he watched Lil' Dru go on a long-range shooting spree, nailing a half dozen three-pointers in his team's win. He granted the occasional autograph request, although most of the fans near him seemed too awed by his almost mythic status to approach. When the game ended, he greeted his teammates and left for the night. He'd be back for the final day of camp, though if he'd known what he was in for, he might have stayed away.

Unlike their counterparts at Nike, the adidas public relations staff allowed media covering the camp unhindered access to the players. As LeBron was technically a "guest" at ABCD and not a player, the adidas PR staff, besieged by requests to interview LeBron, felt compelled to provide a buffer. So, instead of leaving LeBron to fend off a steady stream of reporters as he watched the final day of camp, adidas PR director Travis Gonzolez scheduled a morning press conference, both in hopes of placating the press corps and minimizing the drain on a young man who'd lately had more than his share of media attention. It was a smart idea, but for a number of reasons, it didn't do much to help LeBron's reputation.

Maybe if he had just been on time, he would have escaped the backlash. Instead, LeBron, Gloria, and Eddie were nearly an hour late for the press conference, leaving the media contingent understandably grumpy. Many of them were at camp only to hear from LeBron, ignoring the dozens of future major college and NBA players competing just outside the door, and they didn't like to be kept waiting. Nor did they like it that, when LeBron finally arrived—wearing an adidas headband, rubber Nike wristbands, and a custom T-shirt with KING JAMES printed across the front that he said he "found" in his hotel room upon check-in—he offered no apology for his tardiness. The fact that the press conference wasn't his idea, and that he had no real need to deal with the media but agreed because, at this point, it was part of his "job," didn't seem to matter. To many at that press conference—and, as it turned out, to many more who weren't even there—the kid whose own T-shirt proclaimed him royalty, who wouldn't deny the fact that he was already handling his career like the business it had become, and who refused to feign humility for the same media that had propped him up as a legend, came off as arrogant, entitled, and corrupted. In the following days, those opinions became published "fact."

The reviews were brutal. One on-line columnist—who hadn't even attended the camp, let alone the press conference—played off LeBron's nickname when he wrote that "perhaps he'll need several crowns—he certainly seems to have a head big enough for more than one." His hometown media chastised him for saying there "ain't no good house in Akron," when he explained that he was looking forward to moving his mother out of their small apartment. Of course, there weren't many nice houses in the part of Akron that LeBron and Gloria had spent most of their lives in, and he could hardly be blamed for equating his impoverished surroundings with his hometown as a whole—it was all he'd known. The truth was, LeBron hadn't made his best impression that morning. He joked about keeping the national media waiting on him— which of course they were—and admitted he liked the idea of billion-dollar companies fighting for his allegiance—which of course they were—then quickly realized that such honesty, in many cases, would do him more harm than good.

Not all the coverage was so critical, and one article in particular seemed to offer the most reasonable perspective. "You knew it was coming," CBS Sportsline correspondent and noted grassroots basketball authority Dan Wetzel wrote a few weeks later. "First he's hailed as the 'Chosen One' and the next Jordan and all of that. Then he gets drilled for believing it. So this month LeBron James found himself in round two of the media cycle, this time getting ripped for 'changing,' in some cases by columnists who didn't even attend any of the summer camps and have never spoken to him.

"This kid isn't normal," Wetzel continued, "he is exceptional. People have to stop expecting him to be a typical, aw-shucks 17-year-old . . . As for the media ripping LeBron [for being] a 'changed' kid—no kidding. Who wouldn't be?"

With those words, Wetzel showed a perspective most of his peers seemed to lack. Still six months shy of his eighteenth birthday, LeBron was a single child from a single-parent home who had spent most of his life poor and anonymous in a quiet Midwestern town. Then, in the course of just a few years, he had become a local celebrity and, not long after, a national phenomenon. The media had done much of the work, and while he admittedly enjoyed the attention—thrived on it, even—and while they sold newspapers and magazines with the help of his name and face, he wasn't allowed to capitalize on any of it. The sneaker companies did their part, too, courting LeBron for a partnership that would one day make him very, very rich—but, up to that point, was good for little more than free shoes and T-shirts. Barring serious injury or a total collapse of his game, LeBron's massive payday was most likely less than a year away; the catch was that while amateur ideals technically prevented him from making so much as a penny off his talent, he was already being treated as a millionaire. The shoe companies flew him back and forth across the country, the media put demands on his time and made money off his fame, potential agents whispered promises and introduced him to their star clients—and through it all, LeBron James was supposed to act like the same poor, anonymous kid from Akron, grateful for the attention and content to go quietly back to that small apartment every night. Given all that, the only thing he *could* do was enjoy it, take advantage of the perks where he could, and do his best to make sure no one took advantage of him. And if that mentality didn't make him any new friends, fine—LeBron already had plenty of those.

LeBron's trip to ABCD Camp had one other negative effect: By leaving the state and traveling with LeBron to New Jersey, Eddie Jackson had violated one of the conditions of his release on bond and was forced to put up additional bond money. It would turn out to be the last trip he'd be able to make with LeBron, but as far as the summer of 2002 was concerned, that wasn't a big deal—LeBron had only one more trip planned. In mid-August, he headed to Michael Jordan's youth basketball camp in Santa Barbara, California, to serve as a counselor, and, with his cast freshly removed, to play in pickup games with the select group of NBA, college, and high school players who also worked as counselors. Though the camp was held largely away from the media glare, word got out: LeBron had played well, and his popularity was undeniable. As Maverick, who also worked at the camp, said at the time, "He signed more autographs than Mike."

The month of August was LeBron's life in a nutshell: playing basketball with Michael Jordan in California one day; back home a few days later to volunteer for a youth education rally sponsored by the Akron Urban League; then learning that Eddie had pleaded guilty in his fraud case and was facing a three-year prison sentence. Living out his athletic dream, giving his time for a good cause, and dealing with the adverse effects of a controversy he'd done nothing to create. September brought more of the same as he began his senior year of high school. First came the rumor that Sonny Vaccaro, the adidas grassroots basketball czar who was instrumental in the company's efforts to sign LeBron, might be leaving for a similar role at Reebok. Theoretically, that rumor had nothing to do with LeBron—but given the timing, and Reebok's desire to join adidas and Nike as a player in the grassroots scene, it potentially had *everything* to do with LeBron. Eventually, Vaccaro announced he was staying put, but the fact that the rumor had surfaced at all showed the extent of the stakes where LeBron was involved.

By that time, LeBron had made it official that he would sit out his senior year of football. It was a tough decision, but with wrist (which he'd rehabbed with the help of Tim Grover, Michael Jordan's personal trainer) not quite fully recovered and his financial future essentially guaranteed through basketball, it was unquestionably the smart one. With basketball season not starting until late November, LeBron actually went a few months without making any actual news—and, somehow, his name popped up regularly in the newspapers anyway. First it was Cavaliers' veteran Lamond Murray, who, unhappy with his role on the team, had demanded a trade by telling reporters, "It's so obvious what the plan is—they want more fan support and they want to do it by getting that kid. They're going young, and they'll use that as an excuse while they're losing so they can get that top pick." There was no question who "that kid" was.

Soon after came news that the Cavs weren't the only ones counting on LeBron. In early October, St. V announced its boys' basketball schedule, an ambitious slate that featured a number of nationally ranked teams and trips to Pittsburgh, Philadelphia, Los Angeles, Trenton, New Jersey, and Chapel Hill, North Carolina, as well as games throughout Ohio. The school would collect handsome appearances fees for each expenses-paid trip, one of the first of a series of decisions by the school that would bring accusations of greed and exploitation. LeBron, though, like the rest of his teammates, was thrilled, both at the chance to travel and the opportunity to test themselves against some of the best teams in the nation. With a senior class that featured the Fab Four of LeBron, Sian Cotton, Willie McGee, and Dru Joyce and big man Romeo Travis, the Irish felt they had a shot a national championship. For a number of reasons, the biggest game on St. V's schedule was a matchup with Oak Hill Academy, scheduled for mid-December. It would have been enough that Oak Hill was arguably the top prep basketball program in the nation, and that the Irish desperately wanted revenge against the team that had narrowly beat them twice in the previous two seasons—put in perspective, 40 percent of the Fab Four's losses as high schoolers had come against Oak Hill. But a game that hadn't needed any further hype got some anyway when it was announced that ESPN2 would broadcast the game live. A national, prime-time telecast of a regular-season high school game was unprecedented, and it could have only happened because of LeBron.

Not long after, LeBron found out he and the Irish would be getting more airtime, when the local Time Warner cable distributor announced plans to offer St. V's game to subscribers on a pay-per-view basis. Reaction to that decision, the team's schedule, and the season-ticket plans St. V offered for its home games at Akron's Rhodes Arena came to a head before the Irish had played a single game in their 2002–03 season. Among the national media opinions, a Milwaukee columnist used the pay-per-view news to prove his colorful point that, "We're on the rocket sled to sports hell," while a Philadelphia newspaper writer—one who regularly appeared on TV sports talk shows—opened his column on the evil influence of television in sports with the following prediction of doom: "Now they are after our kids." At issue for most critics was the exploitation of amateur athletes whose talent generated profits they weren't allowed to share. Put on the defensive, St. V administrators explained they were only trying to meet the growing demand of local fans and their own alumni, many of whom couldn't get tickets to see St. V's often sold-out games, and that while they might make some money off the deal, no one was getting rich. Typically, the opinions that should have mattered most—those of the St. V players—were largely ignored, but as just about all those players happily admitted, the thought of having their games televised was just fine with them.

As it was, St. V's first "game"—technically a three-team preseason scrimmage—wouldn't be televised, but it nonetheless drew plenty of attention. Nearly a thousand people turned out to watch a series of fifteen-minute "minigames" featuring St. V, Barberton, and host Brunswick, the sort of scrimmages held to give players a taste of game action before the start of the season. At most schools, sessions like these weren't likely to draw more than one or two dozen fans; but with LeBron in attendance, Brunswick officials distributed free tickets in the hopes of keeping things organized, and the local media turned out in force. Against inferior competition, LeBron played sparingly but spectacularly, dunking and passing with his usual flair and giving those fans lucky enough to get their hands on a free ticket far more than their money's worth.

A week before St. V's season opener, and just a few days before Time Warner officially announced its pay-per-view schedule for all ten Irish home games, the *Akron Beacon Journal* published a two-sided, full-color "commemorative" poster of LeBron in its Sunday paper. Like all other LeBron James collectables—*Sports Illustrated* and *SLAM* issues, videotapes of his games, so-called "rookie" trading cards done without his knowledge or consent, even bootleg jerseys with his number 23 and the St. V logo on them—many of those posters ended up on eBay, where they sold briskly. Resigned to such profiteering on his name, LeBron was intent on not letting that or anything else distract him as the Irish opened their season on November 30 against Wellston High School. Though lacking the reputation or talent-laden roster of many of St. V's later opponents, Wellston boasted a solid, well-coached team that figured to give the Irish at least a little competition. As it turned out, the only thing that gave St. V any trouble that night was the power company.

Playing a rare "home" game in the familiarity of their on-campus gym, the Irish dominated Wellston from the start and held a 45–10 lead in the final minute of the first half—and that's when the lights went out. The local utility company blamed the elements—the region had been hit hard by a snowstorm that day—but the joke in Akron was that all the TV crews plugging into the building's power outlets was too much for the old gym to handle. Whatever the reason, it was hard not to think of the midgame power outage as some sort of omen; of what, though, it was impossible to say. In a few months, it would be hard not to think of that electrical disruption as a metaphor for St. V's season—of a strong, confident team rolling along impressively, only to have some unexpected act interrupt their season-long success. The Wellston Game was never completed; for the moment, LeBron and his teammates were simply worried about their next game, scheduled for the very next day, against an opponent they knew all too well.

The foe was George Junior Republic, the Pennsylvania reform school that had ensured the Irish of their only back-to-back losses of the Fab Four era. Just a week after losing that highly anticipated game against Oak Hill the previous February, St. V had dropped a 58–57 decision to GJR. Eager to get a complete game under their belts and mindful of the outcome in their last meeting, the Irish were a team on a mission as they prepared for their second season opener. The result, a resounding 101–40 St. V win at Rhodes Arena, confirmed that focus. More than just exacting revenge, the victory revealed some telling facts about this Irish team. Their defense, too often porous during LeBron's junior season, had been relentless, as the Irish scored nearly forty points off GJR turnovers. Just as revealing was the fact that St. V dominated a quality opponent without a huge offensive night from LeBron. His line of twenty-one points, fourteen rebounds, and seven assists was impressive enough, but he hadn't been his team's leading scorer—that honor went to junior sharpshooter Corey Jones— and the Irish still won handily. It was only one game, but it was great news for St. V, and more than a little scary for upcoming opponents.

Somewhat surprisingly, the pay-per-view returns on the first two St. V home games were underwhelming, as fewer than a thousand people paid the $7.95 it cost to access the broadcasts. Perhaps the local audience was reaching its LeBron saturation point (by the end of the season, Time Warner would claim it had lost nearly $30,000 on the deal), but that was no reflection on his still-growing national appeal. In those first few weeks of the season, a rumor—later confirmed—surfaced that LeBron would be considered for a spot on the 2004 US Olympic basketball team; the *New York Times* ran a lengthy profile on LeBron on the front page of its sports section; and ESPN2 announced that Basketball Hall of Famer Bill Walton and animated college announcer Dick Vitale would call the St. V–Oak Hill game, which the network was already promoting as LeBron's national TV debut. And, in a prime example of synergy, the new issue of *ESPN the Magazine*—with LeBron on its cover—appeared on newsstands within days of the Oak Hill game.

There was one more obstacle waiting before the Irish got their rematch with Oak Hill—a matchup with Chicago's Julian High, the same school in whose gym LeBron had broken his wrist over the summer. If that coincidence was a motivator, it wasn't evident in LeBron's selfless play, as he totaled fifteen points and sixteen boards in St. V's 75–50 win. Maybe even more notable than the outcome was LeBron's choice of footwear; for the first time, he'd worn Nikes in a St. V game, this pair customized to read "King James 23" on the sides of each shoe. Given how LeBron had flaunted his openness to continued recruitment by the competing footwear makers, his decision to wear Nike hadn't really come as a surprise. It did, however, have industry insiders and media types buzzing about which brand he'd wear in his national TV appearance, which figured to be one of the biggest battles yet in the war for his feet.

Fitting for a game that featured the most hyped high school basketball player ever, the Oak Hill–St. V contest enjoyed arguably as big a national buildup as any high school basketball *game* ever. The controversy, stoked in the national media, over whether ESPN2 was treading on ethical thin ice by broadcasting a high school game only added to the interest. But even if they'd locked out the fans and TV cameras and played in front of an empty gym, the game likely would have been just as huge for those involved. Oak Hill was off to another dominant start, opening the season 6–0 and in possession of the No. 1 ranking in the *USA Today* poll. The Irish, meanwhile, had only two games to their credit—the suspended Wellston game didn't count in their record—but the presence of LeBron and a strong supporting cast on their roster was good for a spot near the bottom of the *USA Today* Top 25. There was even a betting line on the game. And so the stage was set, two nationally ranked teams with a shared history, and the best player in the country there to draw the spotlight once again. Once they got down to actually playing the game, LeBron, as brilliant as ever on the court, surpassed every expectation. His teammates weren't far behind. For the sake of a competitive contest, it was only too bad Oak Hill couldn't come close.

Well before tip-off, the scene at the Cleveland State University's Convocation Center in downtown Cleveland hinted at the scale of the hype surrounding the game. TV satellite trucks, both ESPN's and those of regional stations doing live feeds from the game, surrounded the arena. Nearly a hundred media credentials were issued, a crush that would become typical in almost every St. V game that season not played in Akron. And local entrepreneurs took advantage, charging $20 for parking in nearby lots that usually collected just $5 per car on nights when the Cleveland State basketball team played. Those with money left over after paying for parking could have haggled with the numerous scalpers who lingered outside the gym, charging well over face value for tickets. Inside, St. V students crammed into seats behind one basket wore homemade T-shirts exhorting the Irish, LeBron in particular, and at least two young fans donned shirts with LeBron's *SI* cover image silk-screened on.

By the time LeBron took the floor for pregame warm-ups, ESPN2's demonstrative duo of Walton and Vitale were already working themselves into a lather, heaping praise on LeBron as they would throughout the game, so much so that other noteworthy players on both sides would hardly be mentioned. What would be mentioned were LeBron's shoes—they were adidas, a one-of-a-kind pair of Tracy McGrady's signature T-Mac 2s in green-and-gold patent leather, and they went perfectly with St. V's green-and-gold, adidas-made uniforms, which the company had designed with input from LeBron. Before the season, adidas grassroots rep Chris Rivers had said his company hoped to have LeBron wear a new, previously unseen pair of shoes "about every five games" during his senior season. Counting the Nikes he'd worn in the previous game, LeBron was already well ahead of that pace.

In addition to his eye-catching kicks, LeBron wore a green NBA logo headband, a gold wristband with "Chosen One" embroidered on it that he'd pulled over his right calf—with another on his left arm—and, as always, white sheets of athletic tape over each bicep to cover up his tattoos. That was St. V policy, no exceptions, and many of the Irish players sported similar patches on their arms. On that night, maybe more than almost any other, the St. V players had something else in common: Each played nearly perfect basketball in what was, in many ways, the biggest game of their lives so far.

None, though, played better than LeBron. With nearly twelve-thousand pairs of eyes watching inside the gym and millions more watching on TV—it would be one of the top-rated broadcasts in ESPN2's history—LeBron was at his best. His points came easily and often dramatically, and his intensity dictated the action throughout. He'd always had a flair for breathtaking plays, and knowing full well the reach those ESPN2 cameras gave him, he pulled out some of his finest moves against Oak Hill. Most of his thirty-one points came in impressive fashion, whether drives to the basket, strong post-up moves or long-range bombs, but none was more impressive than the fully extended, cock-back, right-handed tomahawk dunk he threw down on a fast break midway through the first half—a jam so memorable it ended up as a poster in the ensuing issue of *SLAM*. He collected thirteen rebounds, too, along with a half dozen assists, although his best pass of the night didn't set up a basket. Running the break on a two-on-one, LeBron dropped a stunning behind-the-back bounce pass to Romeo Travis; if Romeo hadn't been fouled, he'd have had an easy dunk. It was that sort of play, more than his dunks and athleticism, that showed the kind of skill and instincts NBA scouts coveted—and led the ever-excitable Vitale to exclaim, "I got goose bumps watching that!"

The outcome, anticlimactic as it may have been for the LeBron-obsessed viewing public, was a 65–45 St. V victory. By themselves, LeBron and Romeo had outscored the Warriors, and while it was clear that Oak Hill had been overrated and was nowhere near as good as it had been when Carmelo Anthony led the team a year earlier, it was just as clear that the Irish were much better than the twenty-third-ranked team in the country. Beyond reclaiming the state championship they felt was rightfully theirs, LeBron and his teammates had their hearts set on an even bigger crown; with this win, a national championship suddenly seemed much more attainable. But that was a long-term goal, and like any team following the clichéd but sensible "one game at a time" philosophy, they had more immediate matters with which to concern themselves. For the time being, the Irish, and especially LeBron, would content themselves with what might have been the sweetest win of their high school careers. Asked shortly before the end of his senior year to name the most gratifying basketball moment of his time at St. V, LeBron didn't hesitate.

"I think my senior year, that Oak Hill game," he would say. "Losing to them two years in a row, and being so close—and then being the first game on national television and being able to win by twenty, that was a big accomplishment for me and my teammates."

It was also a monumental moment for LeBron's place in the American consciousness. Before the Oak Hill game, his name had become a recognizable one to even casual sports fans, but the vast majority of those fans had never seen him play. They might recognize his face from a magazine cover, and they might have caught a glimpse of a highlight on ESPN. But all this was far different from the experience of watching him play a complete game—in this case, one he dominated from start to finish, one in which well-known broadcast personalities raved about him from the tip-off to the final buzzer. The media continued to do its part; in a consensus nearly as universal as the criticism he'd heard after his ABCD Camp appearance, LeBron was lauded as a can't-miss, do-everything future star by writers and commentators across the country. There were a few dissenting voices, those who didn't want to buy into the hype or simply refused to give so much credit to a high school kid; but by and large, the praise was universal.

The Irish had just two days off before traveling to Pittsburgh, just a few hours drive south, to take part in the Steel City Hoopla showcase at the downtown Mellon Bank Arena. With a number of Pittsburgh Steelers players in attendance, LeBron scored thirty-two points and added a dozen rebounds as the Irish avoided a post–Oak Hill letdown with an 82–48 win over New Castle High of Pennsylvania. Back home after just a single night off, they faced in-state foe Willard High School; LeBron had thirty-six as St. V rolled to a 103–49 victory at Rhodes Arena. By mid-December, the Irish were a remarkably impressive 5–0, stifling their opponents defensively and scoring almost at will. And it was a team effort on both sides of the ball, with points coming from all over the lineup and their aggressive team defense proving nearly impenetrable. The Fab Four's final season was going as well as they could have possibly hoped. Things hadn't yet started to get interesting.

Chapter Ten

It was a Friday, just a few days before Christmas 2002, and the buzz among Philadelphia basketball fans was that night's matchup between the hometown Sixers and the visiting Lakers. It would be the only visit of the season by the three-time defending NBA champs from Los Angeles, and given the star power on the court—most notably Sixers star Allen Iverson and Philly-area product Kobe Bryant—there wouldn't be a bigger regular-season draw for NBA fans in this basketball-crazy town.

Understandably, given the caliber of the matchup, a top NBA public relations officer had made the short trip down from the league offices in New York, both to catch a big game and catch up with some of its players. She was friendly with virtually every player in the league, especially some of its bigger names, and the quick trip down the New Jersey Turnpike gave her a chance to check in with a few of the biggest. All of which was why she found it exasperating when her cell phone rang, more than once, with calls from coworkers back in New York telling her to be on the lookout for LeBron James. "It was like, 'LeBron's coming to the game! Keep an eye out!'" she recalled that weekend. "I'm down here to see

Allen and Kobe, and they're going nuts over this high school kid. I think we need some perspective."

It wasn't anything against LeBron, who was in town with the rest of the St. V team for a Sunday night game against local power Strawberry Mansion. Though she hadn't yet met LeBron, this NBA exec had heard mostly good things about him, and like any basketball fan, she was looking forward to seeing what he could do when he made his expected NBA debut the following season. But, of course, she wasn't just any fan; she was an insider, on a first-name basis with people like Allen and Kobe and Michael (yes, that Michael) as well as NBA commissioner David Stern. Her perspective took into consideration what was good for both the players and the league, and when her own coworkers treated rumors of LeBron's attendance at a Lakers–Sixers game as celebrity gossip, she worried that the situation wasn't good for the players *or* the league.

"I'm worried about how players are gonna treat him next year," she explained. "I mean, these are grown men, and this is a business—these are their *jobs*. And all they've heard about is how this kid is the greatest thing ever. It's going to be tough on him when he gets up here."

As for the league itself, she was concerned that some of her peers, people who probably should have known better, were getting caught up in the hype machine that had already warped the perspective of so many outside the game. Even if LeBron was as good as advertised, she reasoned, could he actually be that much *better* than Kobe or Tracy McGrady? As good as they now were, these were players who'd struggled initially after making the jump straight out of high school, and neither had worn a target as big as the one LeBron would have on his chest during his rookie season. Maybe he'd one day be better than either of them, maybe even better than Jordan himself, but the expectations—some of them, intentionally or not, coming from the league itself—for LeBron to succeed immediately would be nearly impossible to match. Her biggest worry, she admitted, was that everyone, the NBA included, was setting LeBron James up to fail.

With all that on her mind, the league official had no interest in meeting LeBron just yet—"If he's as good as everyone says he is, I'll meet him soon enough," she said. Symptoms of that hype, which this particular NBA exec had wanted no part in encouraging, had been evident just a few hours earlier, when the St. V contingent arrived at the airport—and were greeted like rock stars.

"There were like thirty people waiting at baggage claim when we got there," Maverick would later remember. "I don't know how they knew what flight we were on." In that sense, at least, it was probably a good thing that LeBron had skipped out on the game after he and his teammates arrived in Philadelphia that evening. Their weekend would be busy enough, with a couple of practice sessions, an impromptu shopping trip or two, and a bit of sight-seeing around Philadelphia's historic downtown area. That schedule had been set up by Jeremy Treatman, a former assistant coach on Kobe Bryant's Lower Merion High School team who'd since entered the promotions business, and who had arranged St. V's appearance in Philadelphia as part of something he was calling the "Scholastic Fantastic LeBron James Tour." The Irish's trip to southeast Pennsylvania marked the first of four LeBron-featured events Treatman would promote during the 2002–03 season.

After relaxing at their downtown hotel Friday night, the Irish traveling party hit the town on Saturday, hitting well-known

Philly tourist attractions like the Liberty Bell and Independence Hall before stopping into an unremarkable storefront on Walnut Street. The smallish shop was home to the Mitchell & Ness Nostalgia Co., a nearly century-old sporting goods company that, decades earlier, had outfitted many of the city's college and professional sports teams. By the 1990s, Mitchell & Ness was known primarily as a maker of vintage Major League Baseball jerseys—pricey, painstakingly detailed replicas that sold mostly as collectibles to middle-aged and older baseball fans. But over the past few years, as hip-hop acts like OutKast began to wear the jerseys in videos and TV appearances—and as Mitchell & Ness expanded its selection to include classic NBA and NFL jerseys—the company went from a small, regional success to a national phenomenon. Allen Iverson had donned a Mitchell & Ness "throwback" Sixers jersey on the cover of *SLAM* a few years earlier, and rappers and other celebrities of the hip-hop generation soon had closets full of Mitchell & Ness gear. The impressionable kids who followed their cues weren't far behind, and by the time LeBron was a high school senior, Mitchell & Ness jerseys were the height of hip-hop fashion.

It was midafternoon on the last Saturday before Christmas when LeBron and the nearly two dozen people who made up the St. V delegation crowded into the small retail space. They were a conspicuous group, tall young men in matching gold velour adidas warm-up suits, and so it wasn't hard for the handful of "regular" customers in the store to tell they were members of a basketball team. Nor was it difficult—given how his face had been plastered all over the sports media of late— to figure out that the tallest kid in the group, the one with a fitted baseball cap pulled down low over his eyes, was LeBron James. Slowly but surely, some of those other customers recognized him; a teenaged shopper, apparently remembering LeBron's choice of footwear from the Oak Hill game a week earlier, whispered to his friend to "ask him for a pair of those adidas." As it was, LeBron and his teammates came and went quickly enough to avoid a scene, staying long enough for a few of the kids to pick up more fitted hats, and Maverick buying two throwback basketball jerseys—one for himself, and one for LeBron. Though it hadn't seemed so at the time, it would prove worth remembering that those jerseys had indeed been paid for.

Back at their hotel a few hours later, waiting to board one of the chartered vans that would drive them the short distance to the Palestra for an early-evening shoot-around, the St. V players congregated in a corner of the lobby. Eyeing them apprehensively from a couch fifteen or twenty feet away, two teenage boys, roughly the same age as the Irish players, sat with copies of the current *ESPN Magazine* in hand. After finding out from a friend that St. V was staying at that hotel, they explained, they'd driven from an hour away, all in the hopes of getting LeBron to sign their magazines. Perhaps too nervous to ask, they missed their chance that night, but they promised they'd be back. The next morning, another young fan staking out the lobby succeeded in getting LeBron to ink a copy of the same *ESPN* issue. As he'd done after the *Sports Illustrated* cover story came out, LeBron had said he wouldn't sign copies of the *ESPN* issue, both because it, too, was making its way onto eBay, and because he and his family had viewed the article as unnecessarily negative. But he signed here, and when a friend standing nearby pointed out that he "thought you weren't signing those anymore," LeBron was almost bashful in his reply. "I'm not," he said. "I just haven't learned how to say no."

This, for anyone who was willing to listen to his friends and teammates or saw him in person, away from a prying media and curious public, was the real LeBron. This was the intense practice player, committed to getting better despite already *being* better than anyone he ran up against, leading by example and barking at his teammates if he found their intensity lacking. This was the overgrown kid whose friends still teased him about his big ears, the often quirky player whose unorthodox free-throw-shooting style—arms extended straight up above his head in follow-through, eyes following the arc of the ball instead of focusing on the rim like most shooters would—left his cousin Maverick mystified that those free throws ever went in. And this was the playful, largely unaffected kid who stayed on the court after shoot-around that Saturday night at the Palestra, giggling through a mock-serious game of one-on-one with a young member of the St. V traveling party, an eight- or nine-year-old kid who couldn't have known how lucky he was. This was the real LeBron, those friends and teammates insisted, the one often overshadowed by the somewhat aloof public persona he'd been increasingly forced to adopt.

Of course, this was also the kid whose rise to national fame would inspire the sort of TV news segment that aired that same Saturday night on CNN Headline News. "The Making of OJ Mayo," a short feature on a Kentucky eighth grader who was already a star on the high school varsity team, made reference to LeBron, and the show itself wouldn't have—*couldn't* have—happened without LeBron setting the precedent. Nor would the Palestra have played host to an oversold, standing-room crowd the next night, a crowd that included Allen Iverson, a handful of up-and-coming rap stars, and even his good friend Sebastian Telfair, all there to watch LeBron once again take center stage. St. V's 85–47 blowout of local favorite Strawberry Mansion High School was the fourth and final game in the daylong Scholastic Play-by-Play Classic, an event that likely would have drawn in the hundreds, not the thousands, if not for the presence of the Chosen One.

After returning victorious from Philadelphia, the members of the St. Vincent–St. Mary basketball team enjoyed a brief return to normalcy, getting five days off around Christmas—though many of them, LeBron included, met up for a casual shoot-around on Christmas night. Three days later, the Irish were scheduled to be back in Columbus, home to some of the biggest games of the Fab Four era. This one figured to be as big as any of them: the opponent was Brookhaven High of Columbus, a team that stood sixth in the nation in the latest *USA Today* poll. Brookhaven's top player was Andrew Lavender, a diminutive but incredibly quick and polished senior guard who was already committed to attend the University of Oklahoma. The Irish, meanwhile, came in ranked ninth by *USA Today,* but their "underdog" status shouldn't have been too intimidating—they had, after all, beat preseason No. 1 Oak Hill by twenty points just two weeks earlier. Both teams brought unblemished 6–0 records into a game that most observers believed featured the two best high school teams in all of Ohio. The game—the second of four St. V contests on the Scholastic Fantastic LeBron James Tour—was played at Ohio State's Value City Arena, a gym the Irish had last left in defeat. It was the site of their loss in the state championship game just nine months earlier, and given the caliber of their opponent on this day, LeBron and his teammates knew they'd have to play well if they didn't want to leave Value City Arena with the same result. They nearly did just that.

After an uninspired start by both teams, the Irish took a

31–24 lead into the half. It wasn't a bad position to be in, except that they'd let most of a fifteen–point lead slip; by the end of regulation, the rest of the lead was gone, as well. The fourth quarter ended with the score tied at 59–59, but St. V needed a bit of luck to earn an overtime period and a chance to salvage the win. Lavender, who would finish with twenty-seven points, had missed a pair of free throws in the closing seconds that would have all but assured Brookhaven the victory. "I thought the game was over," LeBron admitted afterward—only it wasn't.

Granted a second chance, the Irish took advantage and eventually pulled out a 67–62 victory in front of nearly eighteen thousand fans. Thanks to twenty-seven points from LeBron and timely baskets by junior sharpshooter Corey Jones, the Irish had managed to stay perfect, but just barely. Heading into the New Year, and what would be the final three months of LeBron's high school career, they were 7–0 and had staked their claim as quite possibly the best high school team in the country. There would be more challenges on the court—and some unimaginable ones off it—if the Irish hoped to finish the season as impressively as they'd started.

Two days into the new year, and less than a week after LeBron's eighteenth birthday, the Irish landed in Los Angeles for their longest road trip of the year. This cross-country excursion would culminate with the Pangos Dream Classic, yet another high school showcase tournament run by yet another promoter, this one an L.A.-based prep basketball entrepreneur who managed the coup of his career by convincing St. V—and therefore LeBron—to fly out over the holidays. And if four days of near-perfect weather wasn't enough to make them glad they'd left the chilly Midwest, the Irish had the added motivation of facing yet another opponent ranked in the *USA Today* top 10. Their latest highly rated foe would be Mater Dei High, a perennial Southern California power from nearby Santa Ana that came into the game with three Division I college signees, a 14–1 record, and the No. 4 ranking in the latest *USA Today* poll. The Irish, still ranked ninth, knew that a win here, combined with their victories over Oak Hill and Brookhaven, might be enough to vault them to the No. 1 spot. It was just one more incentive to win in what would go down, for many reasons, as their most memorable trip of the year.

The day before the game, the St. V players joined up with the other teams playing in the four-game, all-day showcase— including Brookyln's Lincoln High School, featuring LeBron's good friend and *SLAM* cover subject Sebastian Telfair—at Lawry's, the pricey, semifamous Beverly Hills prime rib restaurant. The occasion was a banquet honoring participants in the Dream Classic, and also gave the media an opportunity to speak to the participants. Of course, the vast majority of that media—including a *New York Times* writer and a reporter and photographer from *Sports Illustrated* who followed the team around most of the weekend—were there for one reason only. For the sake of fairness, members of each team were pulled out of the Lawry's dining room into an adjacent room that had been set up for interviews; the most popular question all of them heard was, "So what do you think of LeBron James?" When it was finally St. V's turn, and Coach Dru ushered all of his players into the press room, his son couldn't help but smile. "Here we go for our LeBron James press conference," Little Dru said with a laugh.

By that time, it was all part of a day's work for the rest of the St. V players, and while Dru's crack about tagging along while his world-famous friend and teammate met the press was sarcastic, there was no bitterness in his voice. As Keith Dambrot had said nearly two years earlier, LeBron had no reason to worry about jealous teammates as long as he stayed unselfish on the court. That hadn't changed, and neither had his status as "same old 'Bron" when the reporters and awestruck fans weren't around. Besides, if it hadn't been for LeBron, Dru and the rest of the Irish knew they wouldn't have been able to enjoy trips like these—not to mention the minor celebrity they themselves enjoyed when people found out they were on "LeBron's team." The Irish supporting players had their names and faces in the local papers far more often than star players on other area teams, and Dru, Romeo, Sian, and Willie had already been featured in a *SLAM* article and photo shoot. Benefits like those, along with the bundles of shoes and warm-ups that came with the team's adidas sponsorship, and the chance to wear nicer uniforms than some NBA teams, more than made up for any negative side effects brought on by LeBron's fame.

That night, a Friday, the Irish congregated at their hotel near the L.A. airport to watch their almost hometown university, Ohio State, upset Miami in college football's national championship game. LeBron had a particular interest in the Buckeyes' success, since he and Maurice Clarett, OSU's star freshman running back, had recently struck up a friendship. Then came Saturday—game day. The Dream Classic was an all-day affair to be held at UCLA's Pauley Pavilion, the same gym in which Coach John Wooden's legendary Bruin teams had dominated college basketball though much of the 1960s and '70s. But unlike the previous eight-team, daylong showcase St. V had headlined in Philadelphia two weeks earlier, the Irish wouldn't be playing in the final game of the day.

Such events were usually set up like concerts, with the local teams serving as opening acts and a big-name team like St. V as the main event; at the Dream Classic, though, St. V would play in the third of the four games. That wasn't likely to have been a mistake, and it wasn't—it was just that ESPN2 wanted it that way. Less than a month after St. V had made its national TV debut, the cable giant was putting LeBron TV back on the air. The ratings had simply been too good to ignore, and with the Irish once again facing a ranked opponent in front of a big crowd, their date with Mater Dei was a no-brainer. St. V was stuck with the earlier tip-off so ESPN2 could maximize viewership on both coasts.

That was fitting, since LeBron James was by then unquestionably a bicoastal phenomenon. The L.A. newspapers had run stories on his pending visit for nearly the entire week leading up to his visit, and Dream Classic promoters—who sold programs with a full-page shot of LeBron on the cover for a somewhat alarming $10 a pop—were expecting a sell-out. A moderate crowd showed up in time for the first contest, but by halftime of the day's second game, Pauley Pavilion was approaching capacity. The St. V–Mater Dei game—and by extension ESPN2's broadcast—was delayed nearly an hour when that second game went into double overtime, and by the time the Irish and Monarchs took the floor for pregame warm-ups, the gym had something in common with so many others St. V had played in over the past year and a half: a standing-room-only crowd. Also familiar was a media contingent that neared triple digits. What was different, or at least far more obvious than ever before, were the contingents that lined the courtside seats on the opposing baselines. Regarding each other coolly from across the court were the basketball brain trusts of adidas and Nike. Most prominently, it was adidas grassroots basketball head Sonny Vaccaro, and Nike founder and chairman Phil Knight.

The quiet showdown between key players from the two sneaker giants was huge in any number of ways. There was the fact that Knight, the eccentric billionaire owner of the world's biggest athletic footwear and apparel maker, rarely appeared so publicly. That he had spoke volumes about just how badly he wanted LeBron adorned with his company's trademark swoosh. Then there was Vaccaro, the man credited with essentially creating the modern grassroots hoop scene and everything—good, bad, and occasionally slimy—that went with it. Vaccaro couldn't claim ownership of a multibillion-dollar company, but given the connections he'd made with virtually every great high school player in America over the past few decades, he was considered by some to be the most powerful behind-the-scenes power broker in all of basketball. Short of Michael Jordan himself squeezing into one of those baseline seats, these were the two best-known and most influential players in the battle over LeBron's feet. Making all that much more compelling was the well-known fact that Vaccaro had left Nike—where he'd been largely responsible for signing a young Michael Jordan to an endorsement deal that would revolutionize the sneaker industry— more than a decade earlier and taken his connections and savvy to adidas, making the fight for LeBron both business *and* personal. It was all worthy of a Hollywood script, and that night, Vaccaro gave it one of its most memorable lines. Greeting Knight as he walked by the Nike contingent, Vaccaro later said, he'd whispered something in his old boss's ear: "Let the games begin."

In retrospect, LeBron's price tag might have gone up five or ten million dollars that night. The jockeying for position between adidas and Nike had grown more heated by the day—Vaccaro would later joke that Nike reps had spent so much time in Akron by the time LeBron graduated, "they'll have to file Ohio taxes"—and this almost surreal gathering had only increased the intensity of the competition. Later that evening, adidas threw a party in one of the ballrooms at the teams' hotel to celebrate the three-stripes-affiliated teams that had participated in the Dream Classic, and that party wouldn't likely have occurred if one of those teams hadn't been St. V. Meanwhile, the guesstimated figure for LeBron's inaugural shoe deal, which had initially been quoted in the media as something in the 20-million-dollar range, was by then regularly mentioned as being worth $25 or $30 million for a five-year endorsement contract—and there was no ceiling in sight. Looking back a few months later, an NBA player agent who had been in the running for LeBron at the time was reminded of those numbers. His assessment, delivered with absolute certainty: "Everybody's guess is low."

Perhaps ironically, on a weekend that added so much to his potential asking price, LeBron played one of his least impressive games of the season. He shot just eight of twenty-four for the game, missing all nine of his three-point attempts, and between his poor shooting and the sense that the referees were giving him preferential treatment, many in the sellout crowd came away unimpressed with LeBron—at least compared to the absurdly high expectations they'd brought with them into the gym. Still, an "off night" for LeBron was one many other high school kids could only dream of, as he finished with twenty-one points and enough rebounds and assists to approach a triple-double. More important, the Irish overcame both LeBron's subpar game and the absence of Sian Cotton, who was playing in a national high school football all-star game in Texas that weekend, to beat Mater Dei, 64–58. The win spoke volumes about St. V's depth and balance, and it gave the Irish their strongest claim yet to the title of Best Team in America.

Back in Akron three days later, the now 8–0 Irish found out their claim had been confirmed: the new *USA Today* Top 25 poll released that Tuesday listed St. V as the No. 1 team in the country. That night, they tipped off against nearby Villa Angela–St. Joseph at Rhodes Arena. The game itself—a 97–60 St. V win—was forgettable enough, but LeBron made sure the nearly five thousand fans in attendance would remember it. Having gone without a single dunk in the win over Mater Dei, he seemed eager to spend some time above the rim that night. He did just that en route to a forty-point night, flushing a half dozen dunks, none more impressive than the third-quarter slam that nearly brought the house down. It came from a different angle, but it was essentially the same dunk— take off, pass between the legs, and jam—he'd used to shut down that off-season pickup game nearly two years earlier. Afterward, he called it "probably the best dunk I ever had in a game."

By mid-January, LeBron and his teammates were in a full sprint toward everything they'd wanted to achieve that season, and with what figured to be their toughest games already behind them, they hardly seemed to be breaking a sweat. The young superstar—short of NBA rookie Yao Ming, he was arguably the most-talked-about basketball player on the planet—was dealing with the absurd level of attention as well as anyone possibly could have, turning down interview requests from David Letterman and the *Today Show* and waiting on a scheduled visit from a *60 Minutes* camera crew as he concentrated on the things that mattered most, right then and there. Given everything he'd encountered—the media attention, Eddie's legal problems, and the challenge of proving himself against top-notch competition almost every night—and how well he'd handled it all, it was hard to imagine that anything could derail LeBron from writing the perfect ending for his remarkable high school career.

Chapter Eleven

The *Cleveland Plain Dealer* reported the "news" on January 10: LeBron James had been seen driving a brand-new Hummer H2; the military-inspired SUV was far more likely to be seen on an edition of MTV's *Cribs* than on the streets of Akron. And unlike the Lincoln Navigator he'd driven occasionally in recent months—which belonged to Eddie Jackson, who often loaned it to LeBron—the Hummer was apparently owned by LeBron.

The question of how a relatively poor kid in a single-parent household could afford a truck that retailed for nearly $50,000—not including the TV monitors, video game systems, and customized "King James" headrests this one reportedly came with—occurred to a lot of people, and at least one of them was Clair Muscaro, the commissioner of the Ohio High School Athletic Association. Eight months earlier, as LeBron and his family jetted back and forth across the country as part of his adidas/Nike courtship, Muscaro had been quoted as saying he was concerned about possible breaches of LeBron's high school eligibility. Any number of things might compromise a student-athlete's amateur status, and in LeBron's case, many of those things had never really happened before. "This is new for us," Muscaro had said. "With the caliber of player he is, a lot of unusual situations come up."

This one—"Hummergate," as some in the local media would predictably dub it—certainly fit Muscaro's description. Thanks in part to relentless coverage in the *Plain Dealer,* the story became and remained front-page news, not only in northeast Ohio, but on sports pages and TV broadcasts around the country. Muscaro, admittedly under pressure from parents and coaches of other high school athletes who saw LeBron as above the high school governing body's rules, promised the OHSAA would investigate; St. V administrators pledged to help out any way they could. Among the media and the public, rumors and assumptions swirled—most prominently, though later disproved, that adidas, Nike, or one of the agents vying to represent LeBron had bought the Hummer as a strings-attached gift. If that was the case, he might have played his last high school game. For their part, LeBron, Gloria and anyone else close to the family said the truck had been an eighteenth-birthday present from Glo, who took out a bank loan to pay for it. Since it was virtually guaranteed that LeBron would sign an NBA rookie contract and a shoe endorsement deal worth a combined $40 million or more within the next six months, that $50,000 loan would have been fairly easy to secure.

Two days after the Hummer "investigation" broke, St. V posted a 76–41 blowout of Detroit's Redford High in Cleveland. LeBron, picking up where he'd left off against St. Joseph with a number of memorable dunks, long-range shots, and pretty assists, led the way with thirty points. He hadn't appeared rattled by the inquiry into how he got his new truck, or by the constant presence of TV crews and news photographers even away from the court. It had gotten to the point that Darrell Hill, the chief of security at LeBron and Gloria's Akron apartment complex, would send LeBron "body doubles" out in the Hummer in an attempt to confuse the ever-present media contingent. Hill, a burly, no-nonsense protector, had even begun traveling with St. V on the road. As it was, LeBron and his teammates continued to play through the latest distraction, rolling over nearby Mentor High two nights later for a 92–56 win. Refusing to be cowed by the scrutiny surrounding him and his birthday present, LeBron toyed with it—literally—by taking a remote-control Hummer out to the middle of the court and driving it around the hardwood floor at Rhodes Arena before the game. He was smiling the whole time, and he hardly had reason to stop once the game began, scoring a career-high and school-record fifty points—most of them coming on his eleven three-pointers, another personal best—in the blowout win. Afterward, though he wouldn't deny that he'd been motivated by the controversy that swirled around him, LeBron credited a local grade schooler with the inspiration for his stellar play. Nine-year-old Davonte Greer had lost three close family members in a New Year's Day house fire. After hearing that story and hoping to do something to cheer up him and his mother, LeBron had brought Davonte onto the court for pregame introductions and given him a spot on the bench during the game. While the "Hummergate" saga raged on, the story of what LeBron had done for Davonte would be quickly forgotten by those who covered LeBron's every move. It hardly seemed fair, but then, LeBron was getting used to that idea.

St. V's globetrotting resumed six days later with a quick trip to North Carolina—yet another stop on the Scholastic Fantastic Tour—for a game against in-state power RJ Reynolds High School. LeBron had recorded a brief video promo for a commercial that ran in the days leading up to the game, and his pitch apparently worked: more than sixteen thousand fans, a record for a high school game in the basketball-crazed state, showed up at the Greensboro Coliseum to watch St. V's 85–56 win. LeBron scored thirty-two points to pace the Irish, who returned home to find their leader's name connected to yet another controversy. After a horrible start to the 2002–03 season, the Cavaliers had fired John Lucas as their head coach. Within a few days of his firing, an anonymous source who was said to be "close to the James family" was quoted as saying LeBron would never play for Cleveland now that Lucas had been axed. It was understandable that LeBron might have been disappointed by the firing of a coach with whom he'd become friendly—the same coach who'd caught so much flak for inviting LeBron to that memorable workout nearly a year earlier—but the thought that a high school kid who had yet to declare for the NBA draft would be bold enough to publicly dictate terms to an NBA franchise seemed a little crazy. But, since every step LeBron took at that point qualified as a headline, crazy was becoming the norm.

Finally, a week later, sanity resurfaced for LeBron and St. V. After posting wins against a pair of local rivals—98–46 over Walsh Jesuit on Senior Night, their final game at the St. V gym, and 82–71 over Buchtel, the school the Fab Four had been all but promised to four years earlier—the Irish got some very good news. On the last Monday of January, nearly three weeks after his Hummer first made headlines, LeBron was cleared by the OHSAA of violating state amateur bylaws. It had taken the better part of a month to figure out that getting a birthday present—no matter how expensive—from his mother was allowable, but at least the issue was dead. LeBron managed to keep his new ride in the news a bit longer, getting into a minor fender bender not far from the St. V campus and earning another few days' worth of headlines. But the worst of that drama appeared over ... which is exactly why he probably should have known something even more ridiculous was just around the corner.

It was nearly two years earlier, back when LeBron James was still a sophomore and Dru Joyce II was still a St. V assistant coach, that the elder Joyce had voiced his concerns about some of the pitfalls his star player might face in the coming years. One of the biggest, he feared, was the rush of strangers who'd be quick to do favors for a soon-to-be millionaire — often with the expectation of having those favors returned down the road. "We see it constantly," Coach Dru said. "Everybody's going to want to be his friend, thinking it'll get them an in."

The folks at Next Urban Gear and Music, the Cleveland-area clothing store LeBron and some friends stopped into the day before St. V's win over Buchtel, most likely didn't have any diabolical schemes in mind when they offered LeBron a sweet deal. Recognizing him when he came into the store — in fact, he'd been in the store before — a clerk apparently offered LeBron a pair of throwback jerseys, and LeBron signed some autographs in return. Maybe he didn't think he was doing anything wrong, or maybe he simply couldn't imagine anyone finding out if he had, and so he agreed. Of course, everyone found out a few days later, when the *Plain Dealer* reported the gifts and the fact that the OHSAA was investigating them. The implication — that someone had called the press about the apparent infraction, or worse, that local reporters seemed to be quite literally following LeBron everywhere he went — left many grumbling that things had really, finally gotten out of hand. The story, which was quickly picked up by the national media, broke on January 30. A day later, LeBron James was told that his high school basketball career was over. In a hastily reached decision, the OHSAA had found that LeBron had compromised his amateur status by "capitalizing on athletic fame by receiving money or gifts of monetary value." The Mitchell & Ness jerseys in question—a Gale Sayers Chicago Bears football jersey and a Wes Unseld Washington Bullets basketball jersey—held a retail value of more than $800, and since no one denied LeBron had gotten them for free, the OHSAA believed it had an open-and-shut case. Like everything else LeBron-related, the announcement made national headlines, popping up, among other places, on CNN.com's front page alongside headlines about the North Korean nuclear crisis and the pending war in Iraq. Opinions in the press, and around watercoolers and on Internet chat rooms everywhere, were mixed: Some thought justice had been served, that LeBron had broken a rule and should suck it up and face the consequences. Others pointed to the hypocrisy of St. V, ESPN, various tournament promoters and—given the increased attendance at state playoff games the past few years—even the OHSAA profiting off LeBron's talent while he couldn't technically make a dime. Still others blamed the media for the whole thing; in the most blatant example of that reaction, the *Plain Dealer* reporter who first reported the jersey controversy was booed and threatened by some fans at St. V's next game. It was a harsh reminder that while LeBron wasn't a media creation—his talent and charisma were the biggest reasons he was so compelling—the media's constant, occasionally over-the-top coverage of him played a big part in making him so big, and in the process helped create many of his biggest headaches.

Whatever else LeBron had gone through over the past two years—the media backlash, the increasing lack of privacy,

even the legal troubles surrounding Eddie, who'd recently begun a three-year prison sentence—he'd been able to work out
his frustrations on the basketball court. That wasn't an option
now, though, which made the situation that much tougher to
deal with. And there was more: St. V was forced to forfeit its
win over Buchtel, the only game LeBron had played in after
accepting the free jerseys and, now, the only mark on an otherwise unblemished schedule. For LeBron, feeling at least in-
directly responsible for what had happened, knowing he'd be
forced to watch the rest of the season from the sidelines, and
knowing his team's state title hopes were all but gone without
him in the lineup, the disappointment weighed a million
pounds. Many outside observers opined that LeBron was actually better off not playing, since he could sign that shoe
deal right away and wouldn't have to worry about an injury
jeopardizing his career; but every one of them missed the
point. Such opinions assumed LeBron didn't really care about
his teammates or their goals; they ignored the fact that many
of those teammates were his closest friends in the world and
had been for most of his life. He was rarely underestimated
as a player, but opinions like those sold LeBron short as a
person. It was adding insult to injury in the truest sense.

As it was, LeBron and St. V weren't without hope. He'd tried
to make amends by returning the jerseys to the store, but the
more legitimate means of salvaging his eligibility, and St. V's
season, was a legal appeal, which was put into motion a few
days later when Cleveland lawyer Fred Nance filed for an in-
junction to block the OHSAA's ruling. In the meantime, while
his teammates, coaches, and St. V administrators defended
him in the press, LeBron and his family turned down all but
one interview request. The exception was Deion Sanders, the

former NFL and Major League Baseball standout who worked for CBS. Understandably, LeBron saw more than a little of himself in Sanders—a fellow former two-sport star who'd also dealt with controversy in his high-profile career—and he was just as understandably fed up with the "professional" journalists by whom he'd felt continually burned. So it was that even before the jersey controversy emerged, LeBron had agreed to let "Neon Deion" interview him in Akron. The conversation took place on February 2, a Sunday, shortly after the St. Vincent–St. Mary basketball team played its first game in nearly four years without LeBron James.

St. V's opponent that Sunday afternoon was Canton McKinley High, a strong team that probably would have known better than to think it could beat the Irish with LeBron on the floor. Instead, he was on the bench, resplendent in a tailored gold suit, soaking up the support from the crowd when he entered the gym, then exhorting his teammates to a 63–62 victory at Rhodes Arena. The rest of the Fab Four—Dru and Willie and Sian—did their part, as did Romeo Travis and Corey Jones, but the toughest load was carried by Brandon Weems. An undersize junior guard and close friend of whom LeBron would say, "Brandon's my brother," Weems took LeBron's starting spot against McKinley. He scored just four points, but given the outcome, every one of them counted.

When the game was over, Akron police and a team of LeBron's own security people kept fans and reporters at bay while LeBron sat down with Deion. The interview, which aired on CBS's *The Early Show* two days later, marked LeBron's first public apology since the whole mess had started. "There's nothing I'm more sorry about than disrespecting my teammates," he told Sanders, adding that he had no idea taking the jerseys constituted any sort of violation, and even claiming the employees at Next had offered the jerseys as a reward for his academic success. That last comment had seemed ridiculous to some, though to his credit, LeBron carried a high-B average at the time. But none of that mattered to the Summit (OH) county court judge who handled LeBron's appeal a day later, and his compromise ruling, while not exactly what either side was looking for, gave LeBron James the only thing he really wanted: a chance to get back on the court. By court order, LeBron would be suspended two games—one of which was the McKinley game he'd already missed, and the other would come in one of St. V's final four regular-season games. Their forfeited victory over Buchtel would remain on the books as a loss, and another court date, scheduled for the final week of that regular season, would determine the final outcome of the whole debacle.

Granted a reprieve, LeBron was invigorated as he prepared for St. V's final out-of-state trip of the season, a weekend visit to Trenton, New Jersey, to take part in the high-profile Prime Time Shootout. It was an event that had already played a key role in LeBron's prep career: A year earlier he and Oak Hill's Carmelo Anthony had dueled in a game that, in some minds, proved more memorable than the NBA All-Star Game played the same day in nearby Philadelphia. This season, the opponent was Westchester High of Los Angeles, a perennial Southern California power on par with the Mater Dei team St. V had beaten a month earlier. Coming in, Westchester was ranked seventh in the latest *USA Today* poll; the Irish, with a loss on their record but still unbeaten on the court, remained No. 1. As for the event itself, there were nearly fifty teams—including, once again, Sebastian Telfair's Lincoln High squad—participating in the four-day tournament, but the fans, media, and even the other teams knew LeBron's comeback would be the biggest story of the weekend. In essence, it would be the only story of the weekend, something LeBron made absolutely certain of when he took the court.

In theory, at least, there might have been a few days in his high school career where LeBron was as good as he was that day in Trenton. Given everything that made the day so memorable, though, that would have been a tough theory to prove. All he did in St. V's 78–52 dismantling of Westchester—played in front of nearly nine thousand fans at Trenton's Sovereign Bank Arena—was score fifty-two points, a career best by two points over the fifty he had put up against Mentor three weeks earlier. Of course, that Mentor game had come on the heels of the Hummer investigation, while this offensive explosion came in his first game back from throwback-induced exile. Both, unquestionably, were statements, and just in case any of the hundred-plus media credentialed for the game hadn't picked up on it, LeBron offered a reminder in a crowded postgame press conference: "If you remember after the Hummer incident, I came back and scored fifty. This time I got fifty-two. If something happens again, I'm going to score fifty-two again."

Though still not entirely in the clear in the court proceeding, LeBron's on-court redemption was undeniable. As always, his motto was "I love adversity," and as always, he'd proven he meant it. Duly inspired, the Irish closed out their regular season in convincing fashion, and the closest thing to controversy they encountered in their stretch run was a report that one of the referees who'd worked the Westchester game was facing an investigation of his own—he had quickly posed for a snapshot with LeBron after the game, drawing heat from the New Jersey chapter of the International Association of Approved Basketball Officials. At this point, all LeBron and his teammates could do was laugh, and keep winning. And they did, dispatching Zanesville High, 84–61, in Akron, thanks largely to LeBron's forty-six points. It marked the fourth time in eight games he'd scored at least forty; perhaps tired from all that point production, he totaled a mere twenty-two points, along with eleven rebounds, in a 73–40 win over Kettering Alter. That game, played in Dayton, was LeBron's last regular-season high school game, so it was fitting that LeBron's final act was a perfect example of the selflessness that made him so great. Given the MVP trophy after the game, LeBron thanked the crowd—then called out teammate Corey Jones, whose sharpshooting had been vital to St. V's win, and handed over the award. The Irish as a team still had a game to play, but as part of his suspension, LeBron would sit out the team's regular-season finale against Firestone. He was hardly forgotten, as St. V chose to retire his No. 23 jersey after the game, a 90–43 St. V win. Dru Joyce scored thirty-one points in the victory, and the Irish stood (officially) at 18–1 as they prepared for the final playoff of the Fab Four era. They would open the postseason on the last day of February against Kenmore High, and while LeBron and his teammates were focused on the now, reminders of his future were unavoidable: In the days before the game, LeBron confirmed his plans to play in the Jordan Brand Capital Classic, one of the three marquee postseason all-star games held each season. LeBron had already committed to the other two—the Mc-Donald's All-American Game and the adidas-sponsored EA Sports Roundball Classic—meaning he intended to play in one more all-star game than NCAA regulations allowed. Playing in more than two such games, NCAA rules stated, would

cost him a year of collegiate eligibility. For anyone still thinking he might go to college, the question was essentially answered.

So, too, were any questions about the team's focus when
St. V opened the 2003 state playoffs with an 84–30 rout of
Kenmore. LeBron scored thirty in that one, then went for
twenty-four points as the Irish defeated Archbishop Hoban,
their crosstown parochial rival, 80–48, in the district semifinals. Four days later, they clinched their fourth district title in
as many years, getting forty-one points and fourteen boards
from LeBron in an 83–56 victory over Central-Hower. The regional playoffs were much of the same: Slowed by a nagging
finger injury, LeBron scored just nineteen points, but St. V's
defense and balance continued to carry the day in an 82–32
blowout of Tallmadge in the regional semis; seemingly still
distracted by a painful, heavily bandaged torn fingernail,
LeBron still managed twenty-five points to lead the Irish to a
69–59 win over Ottawa-Glandorf. The game had been tied at
the half before St. V opened a double-digit lead and held on.

Having achieved another team goal by leading the Irish to
yet another regional championship, LeBron earned a pair of
individual honors in the week before St. V would head back
to the state's final four. First came the phone call from the
Naismith Memorial Basketball Hall of Fame, asking St. V to
send one of LeBron's uniforms to be displayed at the Hall's
new museum in Springfield, Massachusetts. A day later, he
was named Ohio's Mr. Basketball for the third straight year,
becoming the first player in state history to be so honored. A
different sort of good news came that week when it became
clear that the still-pending court date to resolve LeBron's eligibility once and for all wouldn't take place until after the
state playoffs. Though he still didn't know how the judge

would rule, LeBron at least knew he'd be on the court when the Irish played their last game. To no one's surprise, that last game would be the state final.

As had been the case throughout much of the state play-offs, LeBron had a comparatively quiet offensive night (nine-teen points, along with nine rebounds, six assists, and three steals), but his undeniable all-around excellence, combined with St. V's ironclad team defense, was good for a 71–46 victory over Canton South in the state semifinal game at Ohio State's Value City Arena. More than eighteen thousand fans, a sellout, crammed into the gym that Friday night. A few more managed to squeeze into Value City Arena the next day when St. Vincent–St. Mary tipped off against Kettering Alter in the Division II state title game. Confident as they were and still unbeaten on the court in the '02–03 season, the Irish had at least one reason to be concerned: déjà vu. A year earlier, they'd beaten Roger Bacon High during the regular season, then lost to them in the state final. This time, they faced a Kettering Alter team they'd dominated five weeks earlier, and they were better aware than anyone of the coincidence. Once on the court, the underdog Knights did their best to encourage any doubts St. V might have had, slowing the tempo in the hopes of keeping the game low-scoring and, by extension, close throughout; the gimmick worked, as Alter took a 19–14 lead into the half. LeBron scored twelve of those fourteen, carrying the load while his teammates struggled to adjust to the game's snail pace.

Looking collectively more poised in the second half, the Irish caught and passed Alter in the third quarter, then relied on LeBron to seal the outcome in the fourth. Given the cir-cumstances — it was, after all, the last high school game for one of the greatest high school players ever — there was no more fitting ending. He scored seven straight points early in the fourth quarter to give St. V a 34–25 lead, and though the Irish were on pace for their lowest-scoring game of the year, their defense was as stingy as ever. When it was over, Le-Bron's twenty-five points didn't look all that impressive in the box score—except that St. V had only scored forty as a team. More important, Kettering Alter scored just thirty-six points, meaning all the distractions endured and obstacles overcome had been worth the effort. For the third time in four years, LeBron and the Irish were state champions. Asked later which of those three state titles had been the sweetest, LeBron didn't hesitate. "I think the last one," he said, "because we were losing almost the whole game, and my teammates looked at me, and said, 'We're not gonna win this game unless you take over.' And I ended up taking it over and winning the game for us. I think that was one of the biggest games for my career."

Given the outcome, it was hard to argue. A week later, *USA Today* confirmed that game's significance, as it solidified St. V's place atop the newspaper's season-ending Top 25 poll. And while it was arguably too early to put the scope of his unprecedented career in real perspective, there were a few numbers worth noting: In the four-year career of LeBron James and his Fab Four teammates, St. V's overall record was 101–6. Against in-state competition, the Irish had gone 80–2 in the same span; not counting the forfeited Buchtel win, that record improves to 81–1. LeBron, meanwhile, had three Ohio Mr. Basketball trophies and two consensus national player of the year awards to his name, the material rewards for his four-year averages of twenty-five points, eight rebounds and five assists per game. In the history of high school basketball, hundreds of players had been more impressive statistically, but few had won as often, and none had ever left such an indelible mark on the face of sports.

In a final bit of closure, the county court judge who had taken on the case of LeBron's eligibility upheld his original decision, meaning St. V's state championship, and LeBron's hand in it, could not be overturned by the OHSAA. The Irish would have to settle for that forfeit, a manufactured blemish on an otherwise perfect record, but they could handle that. Given everything LeBron and his teammates had gone through, the knowledge that they hadn't been beaten on the court was more than enough.

Chapter Twelve

Just four days after St. V wrapped up its third state championship in four years, LeBron embarked on his anticipated trip
through the postseason all-star circuit. An annual rite of pas-
sage for the nation's top high school seniors, this small but
prestigious collection of showcase events was, as a rule, bigger than any one player. LeBron, as was his habit, proved to
be that rule's exception.

First was the Twenty-sixth Annual McDonald's High School
All-American Game, played at Cleveland's Gund Arena, home
of the NBA's lowly Cavaliers. Unlike most of its contempo-
raries, the McDonald's Game, the highest profile of the postseason hoop showcases, is played at a different site each
year; traditionally, there'd been no apparent correlation
between the game's location in a given year and any of the
players involved. But when the site for the 2003 game was
announced twelve months earlier, anyone paying attention
knew the reason why. That choice had the desired effect: Attendance for the '03 game, played just up Interstate 77 from
LeBron's hometown, was announced at a McDonald's record
18,728.

The McDonald's Game wasn't simply a game, but a nearly
weeklong event that featured slam dunk and three-point-
shooting contests and visits to a local children's hospital

(keeping with the charitable theme, proceeds from the game benefited a local Ronald McDonald House). LeBron won the dunk contest, held two nights earlier on the campus of nearby Cleveland State University, but some in the crowd, apparently thinking the judges had gotten caught up in his reputation, actually booed LeBron's victory. Even in front of his home crowd, he couldn't please everyone all the time.

Of less interest to the fans were the week's handful of loosely run practices that allowed the two teams, divided into East and West squads and including players from around the country, to get acquainted before they took the court. Unsurprisingly for a game whose alumni are more likely than not to play professionally — more than two hundred current or former NBA players were McDonald's selections — those practices were also open to pro scouts, dozens of whom attended. The consensus afterward was that, even on a court filled with the best eighteen-year-olds in the nation, LeBron once again stood out from the crowd. As one NBA scout told a local paper, "He's on a different level from these kids."

He did nothing to change that opinion in the game itself. As expected, 'Bron heard the loudest cheer when his name was announced to the near-sellout crowd during pregame introductions, and by the time he took the court for the opening tip, many of the now-familiar totems of a LeBron James game were in place: star power in the front row (Cavs' rookie Dajuan Wagner, already a friend of LeBron's); the unavoidable presence of shoe company reps (Nike, adidas, and late-arriving but deep-pocketed contender Reebok were out in force); and one-of-a-kind footwear (while the rest of the players wore newer models from game sponsor Reebok, 'Bron rocked a retro pair of Question 1 high-tops, the original signature shoe from Reebok endorsee Allen Iverson, with "L23J" embroidered on the sides.) Less familiar was his jersey number—32, a reference to Magic Johnson, with whom he was so often compared, but not his usual Jordan-inspired 23. The reason: In Jordan's honor, the number 23 had been retired by McDonald's organizers.

Once the ball was tipped, LeBron went to work immediately, dunking for the game's second basket and dishing to teammate Charlie Villanueva for three jams, including an off-the-backboard alley-oop, in the opening minutes. In fact, LeBron averaged nearly an assist a minute in the early going, a sign of his well-established willingness and ability to involve his teammates—and, in Villanueva's case, something of an ironic twist. Earlier in the week, Villanueva, a New-York-City-bred star at New Jersey prep power Blair Academy who was also considering entering the 2003 draft, had answered questions about feeling overshadowed by LeBron. In fairness, he hadn't brought the topic up, nor had he shown any bitterness about LeBron's monopolization of the spotlight, but his comments echoed what most of the other McDonald's invitees must have been thinking. Of course, after the game—specifically, after LeBron's selfless playmaking set up a number of Villanueva's personal highlights—Charlie didn't seem to mind LeBron's presence at all. "With LeBron," Villanueva said afterward, "you know if you run the floor, he's gonna get you the ball."

On this night, good things generally happened regardless of what LeBron did with the ball. He finished with a game-high twenty-seven points and added seven rebounds and seven assists—many of the spectacular, no-look variety—in his East team's 122–107 victory. He also played more minutes and took more shots than anyone else in the game, but given his efficiency (he shot 50 percent from the floor) and his assist total, no one seemed to mind when LeBron was named recipient of the John R. Wooden Award as the game's most valuable player. The award's namesake, legendary UCLA coach John Wooden, was on hand to present the trophy after the game.

To basketball purists, Wooden was unquestionably the biggest name in the building that night, but most of those who bought a ticket or tuned in to the ESPN broadcast were more likely drawn by LeBron's increasing celebrity appeal. And judging by the reaction inside Gund Arena, the arrival of multiplatinum rapper Jay-Z was far more memorable for most fans than the presence of the greatest coach in college basketball history. The iconic rhyme-slinger arrived fashionably late, nearly fourteen minutes into the first half, and settled into a courtside seat next to Dajuan Wagner. In between signing autographs for various fans—including players from the McDonald's All-American girls game, played earlier in the afternoon—Jay took in the boys game and alternately cheered for and chatted with the one kid on the court he knew personally. LeBron seemed to enjoy the attention. And for anyone wondering what brought a globetrotting millionaire rapper to a high school basketball game in Cleveland, Maverick explained, "Jay had told 'Bron he was going to come see him play. Jay owed him, and this was about his last chance."

The Thirty-ninth Annual Roundball Classic, played five days later in Chicago, proved that the McDonald's folks probably would have had a nice turnout even without the "coincidence" of a game staged in LeBron's backyard. Announced attendance for this year's edition of the Roundball—the original high school all-star game, started by Sonny Vaccaro as the Dapper Dan Classic in Pittsburgh in 1965, it's now sponsored by EA Sports and run by adidas—was 19,678, the biggest crowd ever to see a high school all-star game. And just like the Cleveland crowd, this one nearly filled an NBA gym—in this case the United Center, home of the Chicago Bulls who, like the Cavs, owned a decent shot at (and desperate desire for) the No. 1 pick in the upcoming draft. As for the young man most likely to be that pick, LeBron headed back to Chicago hoping for better luck than he had the last time he played in the Windy City. Another broken wrist was not in his plans.

The night before the game, the Roundball players—about half of whom had also participated in the McDonald's Game—along with their families, event sponsors, and media, attended a formal banquet held to benefit the Hoops That Help charities affiliated with the event. The prebanquet cocktail hour included a charity auction, with various pieces of NBA memorabilia, including a signed Michael Jordan jersey, among the items up for bid. LeBron made his way through the crowded lobby where the auction items were displayed, signing autographs for the handful of kids who asked while doing his best to avoid the few obvious autograph merchants—obvious as ever with handfuls of Sharpies and folders bulging with glossy photos, freshly scanned from magazines—who'd managed to sneak into the party. Like all the other Roundball players, he was black-tie sharp for the evening as he eyed shoes, balls, and jerseys signed by the likes of Jordan, Kevin Garnett, and Isiah Thomas. Finally, he stopped an event publicist to ask a question.

"Can I bid on this stuff?"

"Sure . . ." came the tentative reply.

Hearing this, a friend of LeBron's standing nearby relieved the tension. "Just what you need—more expensive jerseys." LeBron just grinned before going off on his way.

Twenty-four hours later, LeBron was once again warming up in front of a packed house, one that was used to larger-than-life basketball stars with "23" on their backs. Jordan's presence on this night was limited to the dramatic tribute statue that stood in front of the United Center, and to the six NBA Championship banners bearing his name that hung from the arena's rafters—meanwhile, most of the No. 23 jerseys in the stands were bootleg St. V "James" jerseys, worn by a number of kids scattered throughout the arena. Current Bulls Eddy Curry, Jamal Crawford, and Donyell Marshall turned out to give the game some low-wattage star power, but even in their home gym, none of them could compete with LeBron for shine. Wearing a pair of patent red T-Mac 2s that weren't scheduled to appear in shoe stores for another three months, while the rest of the players wore brand-new but uniform adidas models, he kept his one-of-a-kind footwear string intact.

At any level, all-star games like these are laden with flashy passing, minimal defense, and an overabundance of dunks, and these back-to-back showcases were no exception. But this year, the difference between McDonald's and Roundball was competitiveness. Where the Cleveland game featured a double-digit margin almost from the beginning, its Chicago rival featured that rarest of traits where all-star games are concerned: a game that was close throughout and featured a down-to-the-wire finish. As if following the same script he'd been reading from all along, LeBron figured prominently in the outcome.

Though his final line was similar enough to the numbers he put up in Cleveland—twenty-eight points on twelve of twenty-one shooting, six rebounds, and five assists—LeBron didn't appear quite as impressive in Chicago. Partly, it was the lack of as many dazzling assists, although his thirty-five-foot, one-handed bounce pass to teammate Dameon Mason early in the third quarter was, without overstating it, as beautiful a pass as any NBA point guard could make. Partly, too, it was a comparative lack of efficiency, from his game-high six turnovers to his o-for-6 shooting from three-point range. Still, even if his effort wasn't quite as spectacular as it had been five nights earlier, his line was solid enough. More important, when the game was in its final minute and the outcome undecided, he made the plays at both ends of the court that, well, decided it. As he told a crowded pressroom afterward, "The first three quarters are for having fun. In the fourth quarter, you have to get down to business."

Despite the fun and loose play, the game was tied 60–60 at the half and 94–94 at the end of the third quarter. But with less than five minutes left in the game, LeBron's West squad (ignore the geographical complications of Akron, Ohio, representing the western US; the lineups were created in hopes of getting balanced teams, regardless of the players' hometowns) suddenly found itself trailing by ten points. And so LeBron, apparently planning his postgame quotes ahead of time, got down to business when the stakes were highest. He had seven points, two rebounds, and an assist in the final 3:51; his highlights included a tough spinning jumper in the lane, a gorgeous pass that found a wide-open teammate for an easy layup, and defensive help that forced a tie-up and gave the West possession of the ball with fifty-nine seconds on the clock. Twelve seconds later, LeBron was fouled, earning two free-throw attempts and a chance to tie the game at 119.

He missed the first, and the crowd, expecting more from the greatest high school player of all time, booed.

Phil Jackson, who coached Michael Jordan's six championship teams in Chicago before guiding Shaquille O'Neal and

Kobe Bryant to three consecutive titles in Los Angeles, once half-jokingly pointed out that Kobe had been known to "sabotage" games in high school, occasionally missing shots or turning the ball over to keep games close so that he'd have a chance to pull them out dramatically at the end. The point isn't that LeBron missed that first free throw on purpose, because he certainly didn't. But, as it turned out, he might as well have.

He made the second, and with forty-seven seconds left, LeBron and the West squad were down a point. The ensuing East possession led to more free throws, this time for East point guard Mustafa Shakur, who stood at the line with thirty-one seconds left, a one-and-one opportunity awaiting.

He missed the first, and LeBron leapt into the lane, pulling the rebound out of the air and immediately turning up court. As much as he liked to pass, shots like these, he believed, belonged to him, and he didn't wait for any help. Dribbling hard and fast down the floor, a single defender on him, he pulled up about eight feet from the basket and shot. The ball banked in cleanly, and with twenty-five seconds left, the West held its first and only lead of the fourth quarter, 120–119. The East failed to score on its final possession, and LeBron James hoisted another MVP award.

Three weeks later, LeBron suited up for his final amateur game, the Jordan Brand Capital Classic held at the MCI Center in Washington, DC. For LeBron, the game was notable because it was his third postseason all-star game—exactly one more than allowed by NCAA regulations. Because LeBron continued to say he was "undecided" about his post–high school plans, and because some in the media were apparently unaware of the NCAA rule, there was still a vague sense that his options were actually open. In truth, LeBron's plans for the summer of 2003 had been a foregone conclusion for months, and when he took the court at the Jordan Game, those plans essentially became official. The lead in the *Akron Beacon Journal*'s game story put it bluntly: "At 8:26 P.M., LeBron James became a professional athlete."

Despite playing with a minor toe injury, LeBron used the Capital Classic as another reminder of how suited he was to join the professional ranks. With game namesake Michael Jordan looking on just twenty-four hours after playing in what he claimed was finally his last NBA game—and with a pair of "King James"—embroidered Air Jordan XVIIIs on his feet— LeBron quickly settled into his accustomed takeover role, scoring thirty-four points on thirty shots, and grabbing twelve rebounds in his Black team's 107–102 loss to the Silver. That performance was good for game MVP honors, but LeBron, with the same selflessness and sense of awareness that had led him to hand a regular-season game MVP award to his St. V teammate Corey Jones, had other ideas. Taking the trophy, he acknowledged the play of Illinois point guard Shannon Brown, who had twenty-seven points and eight assists for the victorious Silver, and basically demanded that Brown share the MVP. Brown complied, and LeBron made sure his final amateur game ended with a reminder that he could be selfless off the court, too.

And with that, although the 2002–03 NBA season was still six months away, LeBron James was free to begin his professional career. Of course, he still had thirty-some days of classes left, and like most kids in the last month of their senior year, LeBron would find himself easily distracted with thoughts of the future. The fact that his future involved a potential nine-figure shoe deal and a trip to New York to take his rightful place at the front of the NBA draft order could only have added to the daydreaming. Already famous, LeBron was about to become very, very rich. Now, all that was left were the details.

Chapter Thirteen

At the end of April, just a few weeks before his graduation from St. V, LeBron James sat for a Q&A with *SLAM* in what would be his only major print interview before the NBA draft. The days following LeBron's postseason all-star tour were relatively quiet, with virtually all media requests rejected by a recently hired public relations rep, and most of the sneaker companies' high-stakes jockeying going on, for now, behind the scenes. LeBron was enjoying the relative peace, happy to hang out with his friends and immerse himself in the present; recent difficulties were firmly in the past, and his blindingly bright future could wait just a little bit longer.

The *SLAM* interview, which would coincide with LeBron's second appearance on the magazine's cover, followed an exhausting two-hour workout at Akron's Rhodes Arena. While high school and college-age kids played pickup games on nearby courts—aware of but generally not in awe of LeBron, whom most of them had seen here often enough—the soon-to-be multimillionaire worked through shooting stations with Maverick, taking jumper after jumper from spots all over the floor. When he was done—the gym's janitors finally had to chase him out so they could turn out the lights and lock up— the adidas "King James" logo shirt he wore was soaked

through with sweat. Asked how often he ran through workouts like these, his answer was enough to dispel any doubts
about his commitment: "Pretty much every day."

Finally settled in with Mav and a few other friends for a
late dinner at a nearby Damon's sports bar, LeBron discussed
his recent past, briefly relaxing present, and wide-open future.
Less than a week earlier, he'd confirmed the universally foregone conclusion by officially declaring himself eligible for the
NBA draft; now, as he devoured three root beer floats while
waiting for his "dinner" to come, he detailed the process that
finally led to the decision. He said he had never completely
ruled out the possibility of going to college, as unlikely as
that seemed, but that a guaranteed financial windfall and the
near-certainty of being the No. 1 pick were too much to ignore.
Or, as he put it, "I think I'm in a position right now where I
can't get no hotter."

He looked back on the past four years, the memorable successes—that Oak Hill win early in his senior year ranked as
the sweetest—as well as the obstacles and distractions, all
of which, he said, had made him stronger. He talked about
his preparation, those daily workouts with the basketball, and
with the weight work he had planned for the summer. And he
looked ahead, diplomatically refusing to say which team he'd
like to play for or (more lucratively) which shoe company he'd
sign with. As it turned out, both decisions would be made—
the former for him, the latter by him—within hours of each
other some three weeks later. But he did address the money,
likely to be $100 million or more once his rookie NBA contract,
shoe deal, and other endorsements were added up, that
would suddenly be his within the next two months. "Oh, it's
crazy!" he said. "I don't even know how I'm going to be able
to react, really. It's a good crazy, but . . . I'm not really think-

ing about it. I'm really excited about the upcoming season, getting to know my teammates and making my teammates better. Hopefully, they can make me better also."

Where his rookie season was concerned, LeBron's trademark confidence wasn't lacking. "I think I'm a lot better than I was a couple years ago, and I think I'll get a lot better," he said. "Now that I'm physically able to play in the NBA, and I'm starting to shoot the ball a lot better, I think I'll have a pretty good first season." He acknowledged the challenges before him—pressure to succeed, unprecedented expectations, and veteran opponents who'd be eager to put an over-hyped rookie in his place—with the simple admission, "You're gonna have your hands full every night." But, as he was quick to add, "I love challenges, and I think I'm gonna be up for it."

April turned to May, and even as the NBA playoffs kicked into gear, the basketball world once again turned its attention to LeBron. While the NBA's worst teams crossed their fingers that the upcoming draft lottery would bring them the No. 1 pick and the rights to the Ohio high school star, the more intriguing speculation centered on the race among the sneaker companies. And what a race it had become, with a third competitor making a late but dramatic entrance. For most of the previous two years, adidas and Nike had only worried about each other as they worked to earn LeBron's allegiance. Rumors of interest from Reebok and And one were generally seen as just that, largely because it was thought neither could afford LeBron's eventual asking price. But Reebok, which had capitalized on Allen Iverson's popularity, as well as the more recent signing of Jay-Z to a signature shoe deal, to strengthen its position in the shoe wars in recent years, had more money—and interest—than anyone knew. The company had hinted at that interest a month earlier, outfitting LeBron with a customized pair of Iverson's signature shoes in the Reebok-sponsored McDonald's All-American Game, but there was no predicting the push the company was about to make.

By the second week of May, rumors of Reebok's abrupt entrance into the LeBron chase were swirling, and all had one thing in common: the company's willingness to put up an almost shocking amount of money, well over $100 million, to secure LeBron's signature. The rumors were justified when Reebok invited LeBron to the company's U.S. headquarters near Boston and made a pitch that climaxed with the offer of a check for $10 million, signed and ready to hand over, from the company's CEO. The signing bonus was tempting, but with adidas and Nike still to make their presentations, LeBron held off. Within days he was in California, this time for adidas to make its case. This was the company that had the longest and closest relationship with LeBron, but as Sonny Vaccaro was never shy about admitting, adidas couldn't compete if Nike (and, now, Reebok) decided to drive the price up indefinitely. As it was, adidas reps still felt they had a shot; though based in Oregon, the company had rented a cliff-top mansion in Malibu, flying LeBron and a sizable Akron contingent to Southern California to hang poolside, soak in the stunning views of the Pacific coastline, and hear the three-stripes' pitch. That pitch included prototypes of what would be LeBron's signature shoe and apparel line, and a presentation that included the bigger-than-sport goals adidas imagined for LeBron. The company saw him as a potential icon, presenting him with phrases such as "Do You Want to Be the Next Superstar?" and "Will You Do Something Bigger Than Basketball?" — phrases that were also plastered on dozens of billboards and bus-side signs all over Akron that week. It was impressive, but as Nike was about to ensure, not quite impressive enough.

By all accounts, the industry giant blew everyone away with its pitch the following week. Having flown a small Akron contingent out to its home turf of Portland, Nike hosted LeBron on its massive grounds and initiated a multipronged assault: high-tech audio/video presentations, models donning clothes and accessories from a potential LeBron signature line, video highlights of LeBron interspersed with those of Nike athletes playing on a big screen, and—most impressively—actual pairs of shoes, allegedly close to a dozen distinct designs, in his size 15 and bearing his initials. Had LeBron been forced to make a decision right there, he likely would have signed with the swoosh.

As it was, there were still a few days before the NBA's May 22 draft lottery, by which time LeBron and his recently announced agent, Aaron Goodwin, wanted to finalize the shoe deal. Within that time, adidas confirmed Vaccaro's long-held hunch that LeBron's price tag would ultimately be too high, and the company pulled itself out of the running. That left Nike and, surprisingly, Reebok, which stood as the high bidder and suddenly appeared poised to sign LeBron. And by all accounts, Reebok would have done just that if confusion over contractual details hadn't appeared in the final hours of the negotiations. As it happened, Nike essentially matched Reebok's money, and with a superior presentation and a longer history with LeBron, was able to close the deal. The terms, as released, were $90 million over seven years and included a $10-million signing bonus. He'd also signed an endorsement deal with Upper Deck, the trading card company, and less than twenty-four hours before his immediate playing future would be confirmed in the draft lottery, eighteen-year-old

LeBron James was worth just shy of $100 million.

And then he was a Cleveland Cavalier. It wasn't official, of course, but when the Cavs capitalized on their NBA-worst record to earn the right to the No. 1 pick, there was little doubt about whom they'd use that pick on. If there had been, it was immediately erased when Cavs owner Gordon Gund held up a number 23 Cavs jersey with "JAMES" on the back. It wouldn't be completely official until the draft itself was held in late June, but everyone knew what many in Northeast Ohio had been praying for months: LeBron would be staying at home. Nearly two weeks later, the Cavs hired respected former Hornets coach Paul Silas to fill their head coaching vacancy, a move most agreed would be good for the team as a whole, and especially for the team's soon-to-be top draft pick.

LeBron spent the rest of June tending to the details and demands of his new career, including a trek to Chicago for NBA-mandated pre-draft interviews and a short trip to New York City that included a quick media blitz—appearances on MTV and HBO, a photo shoot for *GQ*—and an appearance at the grand-opening party for the 40/40 Club, the upscale New York City sports bar and lounge owned by his good friend Jay-Z. He was back in the Big Apple a few days later when Jay-Z hosted a party for LeBron at 40/40 to celebrate the NBA's new No. 1 draft pick. Finally, it was official, and all the drama, controversy and hard work had quite literally paid off.

Questions. Despite everything he'd been through and everything he'd already proved, a seemingly endless line of questions trailed LeBron James as he entered the summer of 2003, his last before becoming an honest-to-goodness NBA player.

Where would he play? That depended largely on Silas, his

new coach, who was expected to try LeBron as a point
guard—potentially making him the team's primary ball-
handler and floor leader—as well as shooting guard and small
forward. There was little doubt he could play any of the
above, but where he was most suited, and where the team
needed him most, were yet to be determined.

What would the Cavs do to help him? As good as LeBron
was expected to be, the NBA was far too competitive for one
player to completely turn around a bad team—and that's exactly what the Cavs were in the season before LeBron's arrival. What they'd do with their additional draft pick, and any
trades or free agent signings they might make during the off-
season, would go a long way in determining how much of an
immediate impact LeBron's arrival could have.

Could he be a bust? It was a question many were asking,
even if few were actually expecting LeBron to be anything less
than very good as he began his NBA career. Because he
wasn't a player who relied solely on athleticism, and one
whose versatility and intelligence were two of his biggest
weapons, it seemed unlikely that he'd simply fail. But given
the pressure, nationally and especially in northeast Ohio, of
fans and media counting on him to single-handedly resurrect
the Cleveland franchise, LeBron's biggest challenge might
have been overcoming expectations. Even if he was very good
as a rookie, anything short of jaw-dropping greatness figured
to leave some observers disappointed. Of course, where
LeBron was concerned, expectations were nothing new.

Can he handle losing? This might have been the most ap-
propriate question, because losing, at least his team's short-
term failure to contend for a playoff berth, seemed a likely
reality. As much as LeBron had dealt with in his life—poverty,
family instability, controversy, negative perceptions, and harsh

media attention—he'd never really had to deal with losing on any consistent basis. His high school team had won well over 90 percent of its games in his four seasons, and his teams had generally dominated on the AAU circuit as well. It wasn't inconceivable to think that LeBron might lose more games in one NBA season than he'd previously lost in his entire life.

There were other questions, like how he'd handle the increased celebrity and media attention or the grueling travel schedule and number of games that were a part of every NBA season. There were those, like an unnamed NBA executive, who worried aloud that the reluctance of LeBron's handlers to deal with the media—justifiably, in many cases, because they'd been burned often enough—might cause a backlash that would taint his reputation before he'd even played a game. And there were a few who expected—even seemed to be rooting for—LeBron to fall on his face, including the ESPN.com columnist who boldly predicted, "the best King James can ever be is an average NBA player."

The answers to all those queries will come soon enough. What was known, beyond any sliver of a doubt, was that LeBron was as ready for all of this as anyone has ever been and could ever be. Whatever the future holds, on or off the court, no one had ever been through so much at such a young age. No one had ever been more prepared. No one had ever faced bigger expectations, and no one had already met so many. What is certain was that in basketball, and maybe even in all of sports, there has never been anyone quite like LeBron James; and because of everything that happened to him, around him, and because of him, there probably won't be anyone like him again.

Acknowledgments

I'm not sure which is more surprising: the fact that I overcame my well-honed sense of procrastination to actually finish this book, or the number of people without whose help I wouldn't have come close. Judging by the following list, I'll go with the latter—and do my best to thank them all. If I forget anyone, I'm sorry. I'm an idiot.

First, to Michele—sorry about all those 9–5 shifts (P.M. to A.M., I mean), and for turning the futon into an office space. We haven't been married very long, but I think I made the right choice.

To my family—Mom (who gave me a love of reading and a passion for writing), Dad (who taught me about sports, hard work, and the importance of attitude), Yvonne, Whitney, Ashley, Tiffany, Josh, my grandparents, and the extended Jones, Killpack, Lynn, Marchetti, and Lee families. Your support is invaluable—as were all those pre-orders on Amazon.

To the *SLAM* crew—Russ (an underrated still-life photographer, and not a bad editor-in-chief), Susan (who must've majored in jpegs), Lang (good looking on those links), Ben (writing books is hard . . .), and Khalid (destined, I know, to pen that long-awaited Larry Kenon bio.) Also to Melissa, Ivan,

Sally, and (especially) Andrea for huge assists in the photo realm.

Speaking of which, the work of photographers Atiba Jefferson, Clay Patrick McBride, and Jennifer Pottheiser is worth a lot more than what they charged me for the use of their images in this book. Your generosity kept me from actually losing money on this thing, something I very much appreciate.

To Dan and everyone at Levine/Greenberg, for allowing me to convince you, and to Marc and everyone at St. Martin's Press, for making this much easier than it probably should've been. Special thanks to Barbara Cohen, who somehow made hours-long discussions about legal minutiae enjoyable. Also on the practical tip, thanks to esteemed pop culture dissector Chuck Klosterman for proposal guidance, and to friendly neighbor Jim D'Sidocky for contractual reassurance. As I write this, I believe I still owe you dinner.

For inspiration: to the Big 5—Gordie, Ween, BJ, and Damian Andrew Dobrosielski, aka LaSalle—and to Chad and Max, good friends whose steady stream of doubt-inducing phone calls were just what I needed. Thanks, too, to the rest of the PSU/*Collegian* crew; you know who you are. Our collective genius may never be understood, and this is probably for the best.

For opportunities: to Mark and the rest of the overworked staff at *Blue White Illustrated*; Neil, Paul, the 'Shaks, and the other very good people at the *Citizens' Voice*; and Rob and Barbara at the *Record*, both of whom were far too good to me.

And for the topic at hand: to Travis and Rivers, the list of specifics is way too long for inclusion here, but clearly, this doesn't happen without you; and to those in the NBA office and in the player representation field who shared invaluable insights on the players and the process. Told you I could keep a secret.

Finally, to Akron: Randy, Miquel, Rich, Frankie, and anyone else who was cool whenever I came through; Ann Garber and "Chief" Darrell Hill, for helping when you didn't have to; Chris Dennis, for history lessons and some great souvenirs; the St. V coaching staff, especially Keith Dambrot and Dru Joyce II, and the Irish players, especially Dru, Sian, Willie, Romeo, Corey, and Brandon, for letting me tag along. And to Maverick, the man who makes things happen—thanks for keeping me connected.

Which leaves the fam. I'll never forget listening to Gloria James, who'd already been burned by a lot of people she thought she could trust, express her doubts on the day I first told her about this book. This is not, technically, an "authorized" biography, but because I was fortunate enough to get to know LeBron and his family, it was important to me that they knew about it and, for lack of a better word, approved. Gloria's final question to me that day was simple: "Is this something you really want to do?" I said it was, mostly because I felt I could do a good—and fair—job. I hope I have, and I thank Glo and Eddie for the green light.

And LeBron? I like him, which is probably obvious from the preceding 60,000 words. From everything I've seen, he's both a nice, cool, funny kid and an incredible athlete with the potential for true greatness. To him I say thanks—mostly for being himself, as well as for letting me hang around long enough to document a few key moments in his already remarkable life.

—RYAN JONES
New York,
June 2003